The World That Shaped the New Testament

Calvin J. Roetzel

Foreword by David L. Tiede

John Knox Press
ATLANTA

Library of Congress Cataloging in Publication Data

Roetzel, Calvin J.
    The world that shaped the New Testament.

    Bibliography: p.
    Includes index.
    1. Bible. N.T.—History of contemporary events, etc.
2. Christianity—Origin. I. Title.
BS2410.R68 1985   225.9'5   85-12492
ISBN 0-8042-0455-1

© copyright John Knox Press 1985
10 9 8 7 6 5 4
Printed in the United States of America
John Knox Press
Atlanta, Georgia 30365

Foreword

The Bible bridges many worlds, reaching from the setting of our experience back to the context of its origins. Meanwhile the formation, collection, and commentary on biblical texts have been ongoing, and the Bible continues to be read in cultures quite alien to our own. Most Bible readers are aware of only "now" and "then," and they may wonder what they can know about that past, or if they should even explore that history.

For many, the long history of the biblical text is unimportant. It is the book of the present age, and its use ranges from the profound to the trivial. It is the book of the contemporary church and synagogue. The Bible is at home in present communities of worship, in family prayer and ritual, in political speeches and motel rooms. It is used in administering solemn public oaths, and carried for good luck. It is handed out in tracts by street evangelists and bound in fine leather with gold lettering for great cathedrals. It is a source of comfort for the discouraged and of direction for the faithful. Yet this "Holy Bible" may belong so completely within the culture that it simply gives voice to shared convictions. As long as present values are unquestioned, little urgency may be felt to search out the origins of the Bible or to trace its history of interpretation. But challenges to the usage and meaning of the Bible may come from several directions.

Political candidates with opposing views appeal to the same Bible for support. Biblical concepts like "justice," "peace," or "freedom" may carry a vastly different sense in the public speech of South America than they convey in traditional public worship in Western Europe or the United States. Such profound differences in understanding may lead us to renewed study of these sacred texts within their own social, cultural, and historical context in order to allow the texts to speak with their voice and not ours. Then we are compelled to ask about how the Christians and Jews of the first century of this era were also affected by the political realities and rhetoric of the hellenistic kingdoms? What difference did their situation make to their understanding of the "kingdom of God," their vision of history, their experience of historical

terror, and their convictions about their role as God's people in the develop-
ing cosmic drama?

Challenges to accepted biblical understanding may also come from
within the religious community. New forms of religious expression may confront the faithful with convictions and behavior which appear to be as sincere
as they are strange. How can such differing pieties arise from the same religious heritage? What variety can the faith tolerate? Once again, the historical
question may be raised. What social, cultural, and theological factors contributed to the diversity of early Judaism and Christianity? How have such
differences been resolved in the past? Which modern piety more accurately
reflects the tradition to which all appeal? Now the historical questions have
become urgent: what did happen then? can we know? how much can we
know?

Synagogues and local congregations, temples and cathedrals, bishops and
high priests, liturgies, rituals, and festivals continue from generation to generation until disrupted. Once the course of the institution is deflected, a
whole series of questions arise. What is the importance of these institutions?
What is the meaning of the Scriptures? Which writings are sacred? And
which of those are most urgent and authoritative? What fundamental convictions remain about God's presence and action and speech in this world?
How has the world view of the ancient biblical authors influenced our deepest myths and visions of good and evil, heaven and hell, the divine and
demonic?

These challenges from within and without constantly press the religious
community to search for its roots. They also confront all who draw upon the
Bible for interpreting the human situation with the need to seek new insight
and fresh wisdom for living in an altered world. Basic to such a search is the
task of viewing the New Testament in its world, before using it to interpret
ours.

The World That Shaped the New Testament will open the eyes of the
Bible reader both to the world of origins of Christianity and Judaism and to
realities of the world in which the Bible is now being read. Calvin Roetzel is
an accomplished interpreter of the New Testament in its historical setting,
and he is a gifted teacher with an uncanny sense for what will prove interest-
ing, important, and challenging to thoughtful students. He selects his stories
with scholarly understanding and tells them with insight and dramatic art.
Sweeping through the vast reaches of several centuries of Jewish history and
culture within the Greco-Roman world, he lingers with the fascinating Alexander the Great and his prowess, illuminating the theocratic claims of
hellenistic kingship in concrete, vibrant, and frightening detail. He introduces the rich variety of Jewish religious groups and institutions and then
pauses in the complex workshops of their scriptural interpreters. He draws

the reader into the soul of Jewish and Christian belief, demonstrating how fundamental symbols, myths, and visions took shape within the influences, challenges, and perils of the hellenistic world.

The World That Shaped the New Testament will interest all who are ready to consider the Bible as coming from a world that is not their own. Christians may be especially intrigued by the wealth of religious, social, and political comparisons which enhance their reading of the New Testament. Jews may be gratified or surprised by the way the early Christian movement is presented within the spectrum of Jewish faith and history. Other students may be intrigued by the detail and clarity with which this book introduces them to the religious heritage of a people in an ancient vassal state who had been conquered but not defeated. This human story which surrounds the New Testament in its origins may even prompt and direct a fresh reading of the Bible itself.

—David L. Tiede
Luther/Northwestern Seminary
St. Paul, MN

Preface

Evidence heretofore buried adds almost daily to our knowledge of the first-century Mediterranean World. Indeed, technical studies treating Judaism, early Christianity, and the Greco-Roman world abound—scholarly labors which have made this synoptic effort possible. From these efforts have come two solid gains: (1) proof of the diversity of first-century Judaism, and (2) evidence of pervasive hellenistic influence in the Mediterranean World. These excellent technical studies are fundamental, my aim, complementary; I seek the thread running through this baffling complex. I seek to view the evidence as an intelligible whole looking for ways in which the whole is taken up into the self-understanding and self-definition of the early church. I hope to make the fruits of this effort available in nontechnical language to the student who is seriously studying these materials for the first time, as well as to the reader who wants merely to review the evidence.

The New Testament is more than the expression of creative individuals, though it is that, more than a response to a holy figure, though it is that also. It is a record of the shaping of Christian consciousness, a consciousness shaped at many different levels by powerful forces set in motion by Alexander the Great which continued into the Roman period. That mingling of worlds let loose by Alexander permanently changed the face of all middle-eastern culture. No form of religious expression remained untouched, no tradition of scriptural interpretation insulated from those earth-shaking events. No institution was isolated from those pressures, either, and no mythic formulation totally divorced from that reality. This book is written for students who seek a fuller understanding or reassessment of the way the New Testament writers interacted with that world. When viewed in its natural setting it is easier to grasp the dynamic character of the New Testament itself. In addition it is also important to appreciate this environment on its own terms, and not merely as an expendable background whose only purpose is to display early Christianity to best advantage. This world was far more than background, it was also the homeground and foreground of the early church. Its symbols, language, and forms were appropriated and revalued as the early church struggled to frame its message.

The proclamation of Jesus as the Christ did influence the way the New Testament authors envisioned their world, but that world itself gave the church its own language and literary forms for expressing that belief. Its Scriptures were Jewish; its language, Greek; its urban setting, hellenistic; its political and legal forum, Roman—and its mythology of evil a curious blend of each. Thus all were integral parts of the world that influenced these writers and their audience.

Discussions here of the major political, social, cultural, and religious realities of the New Testament writers and the church are necessarily limited. Technical digressions and methodological considerations are purposely avoided. Much that is included will be common knowledge to the seasoned biblical critic, and omissions will undoubtedly be apparent to the trained eye. Yet I have tried to map the major features of the first-century landscape so that the student may be able to view the whole, and through the whole gain new perspective on and insight into each part.

One of the special joys of writing a book is being able to thank publicly those who have offered encouragement and valuable assistance in its creation. The usual caveat applies here also. The mistakes and omissions are mine, but the credit due for any strengths of the book must be shared. Space does not permit me to acknowledge all who deserve to be thanked for their useful contributions. Valuable financial support came from a grant by the Bush Foundation to Macalester College and from a stipend generously donated to me directly by the *Deutsche Akademische Austauschdienst* of West Germany. A special debt is owed to Professor Martin Hengel and the staff of the Institutum Judaicum at the Universität Tübingen for use of the resources of that institute and for other valuable assistance. The editorial staff of John Knox Press has been more than patient with me as the completion of this project was delayed time and again. I am especially grateful to Joan Crawford and Tom Pierce for their untiring assistance and many valuable suggestions. David Rhoads collaborated in the early phases of the project and offered invaluable guidance. Lloyd Gaston and Peter Richardson read the manuscript in its final stages and made substantive suggestions that greatly improved the work. James Stewart and Jeffrey Nash, two colleagues at Macalester in history and sociology, patiently listened on many long runs, winter and summer, and gave good advice on everything from bibliography to title. All of these and others have given valuable assistance. However, a special debt I owe to David Tiede and Diane Wesman. From inception to conclusion David gave valuable time to discussing the project. And both he and Diane read multiple versions of the manuscript, gave them painstaking critiques, and always offered fresh, insightful, informed appraisals. Their encouragement and candid suggestions offered with good humor and grace account in significant measure for the character of the book. Without their assistance the substance of the book would have been considerably diminished.

—Calvin J. Roetzel
St. Paul, MN

Chronological Table

JEWISH HISTORY

B.C.E.

597 First deportation of Jews to Babylonia

587 Fall of Jerusalem, second deportation, destruction of the temple

538 Cyrus issues edict allowing Jews in exile to return to Palestine

520–515 Temple rebuilt

323–200 Judah under the Egyptian Ptolemaic Kingdom

200 Palestine comes under Seleucid (Syrian) rule

168 Maccabean Revolt

142 Judah wins independence

142–63 Descendants of Maccabean family (the Hasmoneans) rule

63 Roman commander, Pompey, occupies Syria and captures Jerusalem

MIDDLE EASTERN HISTORY

B.C.E.

605 Rise of the Babylonian Empire

604–561 Rule of Nebuchadnezzar

539 Fall of Babylon to Persia

336–323 Conquests of Alexander the Great

200 Seleucids defeat Ptolemies at Panais (Northern Palestine)

175–163 Rule of Antiochus IV (Epiphanes)

48 Julius Caesar defeats Pompey

44 Julius Caesar assassinated

37–4	Palestinian region ruled by Herod the Great with Roman patronage	31	Octavian defeats Mark Anthony at Actium
4–39 (C.E.)	Galilee and Perea ruled by Herod's son Antipas	27	Rule of Octavian (Augustus Caesar)
4–34 (C.E.)	Northern Transjordan region ruled by Herod's son Philip		
4–6 (C.E.)	Judea, Idumea, and Samaria ruled by Herod's son Archelaus		
C.E.		C.E.	
6–41	Judea, Idumea, and Samaria ruled by Roman procurator	14	Tiberias Caesar
		37	Gaius (Caligula)
		41	Claudius
41–44	Judea, Idumea, and Samaria ruled by Jewish rule of Herod Agrippa		
44–66	Judea, Idumea, and Samaria ruled by Roman procurator	54	Nero
66–70	Roman-Jewish War and destruction of Jerusalem (70)	68	Galba, Otho, Vitellius
		69	Vespasian
73	Fall of Masada	79	Titus

Alexander's Empire

Taken from J.R. Hamilton, *Alexander the Great* (London: Hutchinson Publishing Group Ltd.), pp. 166ff. Used by permission of the publisher.

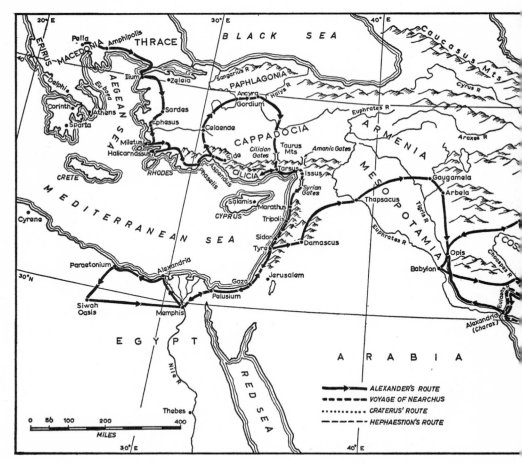

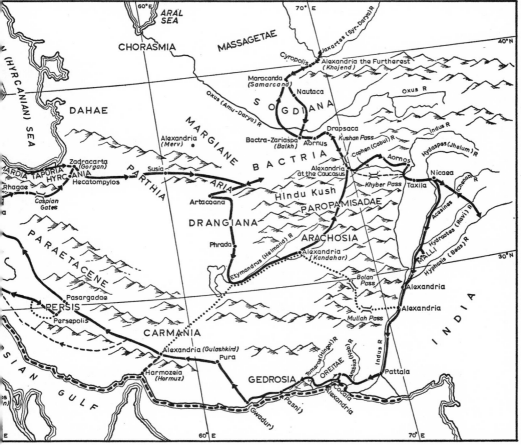

Alexander's Empire

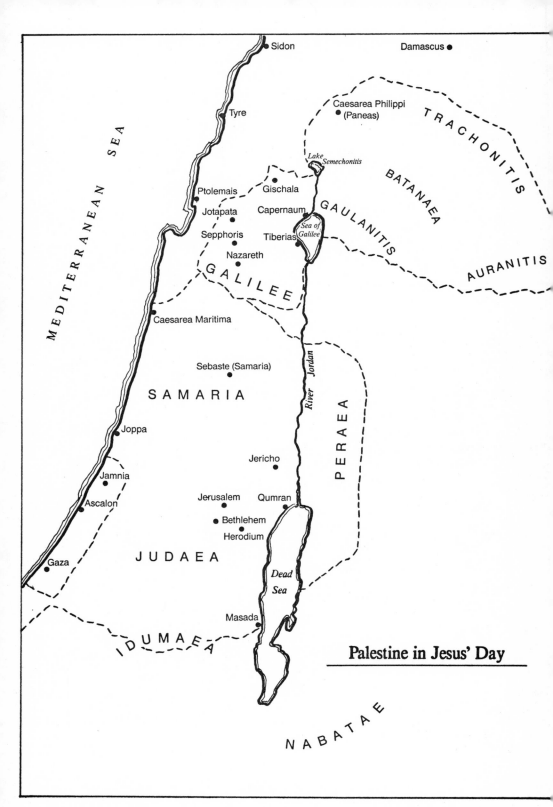

MEDITERRANEAN SEA

Sidon
Damascus

Tyre

TRACHONITIS

Caesarea Philippi
(Paneas)

BATANAEA

Lake
Semechonitis

Ptolemais
Gischala

Jotapata
Capernaum
GAULANITIS

Sepphoris
Tiberias
Sea of
Galilee

Nazareth
AURANITIS

GALILEE

Caesarea Maritima

River Jordan

Sebaste (Samaria)

SAMARIA
PERAEA

Joppa

Jericho

Jamnia

Jerusalem
Qumran

Ascalon
Bethlehem
Herodium

Gaza

JUDAEA

Dead
Sea

Masada

IDUMAEA

Palestine in Jesus' Day

NABATAE

CONTENTS

This book is for
Lisa, Frank, and Mary

Chapter 1

Political Setting

Any person in our world whether from South Africa or Australia, from Nicaragua or El Salvador, from East or West Germany, from the U.S.A. or the U.S.S.R. must view the world through a political lens. Political forces beyond our control impinge on our lives, shape our common destiny, and limit our choices.

In the New Testament as well, references to political realities leap from almost every page. "Whose image and inscription is this?" Jesus asks, staring at a Roman coin. "Are you the king of the Jews?" Pilate, the Roman procurator, demands of Jesus at his trial. The public charge against Jesus leading to his crucifixion was a political charge. The Gospels speak of the High Priest, the Herodians, the Sadducees, false Messiahs, and Roman soldiers. We see references to taxes, war, conscription, royal edicts, and trials. All were a part of the political scene framing the Gospel story. Even Jesus' proclamation, "The Kingdom of God is at hand," called up a rich complex of political associations to the first-century Palestinian.

Paul urged his listeners in Rome to submit to the governing authorities. On the other hand, the author of Revelation exhorted his addressees to resist the idolatrous demands of a demonic state. From this small sample we can see how intimately the New Testament was linked with the politics of the day. Because they were common knowledge, however, these writings describe few of the political trends of the time. For those unfamiliar with the political forces in the New Testament background a historical sketch will be useful. Since the two major political constellations behind the New Testament were Greek and Roman, and Judah existed as a satellite to those systems, our attention will focus on the way these forces influenced the direction of Israel's faith and the shaping of the Christian consciousness.

The Hellenistic World

An abundance of archeological evidence now shows how subtly pervasive Hellenism was in the Israel of Jesus' day. At Caesarea Maritima, for example, one sees Greek styled columns. At Beth-shean Greek inscriptions and art appear. In Jerusalem itself Greek arches abound. To appreciate the lure of Hellenism and its roots in the Middle East one must go back to the time of Alexander the Great, surely "one of the supreme fertilising forces of history."[1] A patron of the sciences, an adventurer bent on spreading Greek civilization, a visionary dedicated to elevating the claims of *oikoumene*—the whole inhabited world—over narrow sectarian interests, Alexander internationalized commerce, established a network of routes from Egypt to India and sprinkled cities throughout Asia to radiate Greek culture.[2] In the words of W. W. Tarn:

> when at Opis he [Alexander] prayed that Macedonians and Persians might be partners in the commonwealth and that the peoples of his world might live in harmony and in unity of heart and mind, he proclaimed for the first time the unity and brotherhood of mankind. . . . Above all Alexander inspired Zeno's vision of a world in which all men should be members one of another, citizens of one State without distinction of race or institutions, subject to and in harmony with the Common Law immanent in the Universe, and united in one social life not by compulsion but only by their willing consent, or (as he put it) by love.[3]

The accuracy of this highly idealized portrait broadly stroked by Tarn is now widely challenged; few, however, dispute his claim that Alexander permanently changed the Middle East. Let us recount in some detail, then, some of the major deeds of this revolutionary figure.

Eager to educate his thirteen-year-old son in the classical tradition, Philip, ruler of Macedonia, lured Aristotle to his court to tutor Alexander. Although he may have comprehended little of the profundity of Aristotle's thought, from the philosopher Alexander did learn about the greatest painter and sculptor of the day (Apelles and Lysippus), about the methods and importance of science, and about the traits of an ideal leader. Like all good students, however, Alexander contradicted his master at points. "Barbarians" (i.e., all non-Hellenes), for example, he thought were not meant to be slaves of the Greeks.

At sixteen, while serving as regent of Macedonia in his father's absence, he successfully quelled a revolt in the border regions of Thrace and Paeonia. At eighteen he led the heavy cavalry on the left wing for Philip in a decisive battle against the Theban-Athenian alliance. Consequently, when Philip was assassinated Alexander at age twenty already possessed the skills necessary to assure his success. Moreover, he inherited a well-trained army, superior weaponry, and a corps of experienced, able, and exceedingly loyal commanders. He carried with him an intelligence unit without peer in the ancient world. His corps of engineers was experienced, ingenious, and resourceful. His surveyors, who made maps essential to territorial control, were able. In addition gifted scientists, architects, historians, and philosophers were also a part of his entourage.

After Philip's death Alexander used his first two years in office to secure the support of Thessaly and Athens in the south and to establish the boundaries of Macedonia in the north up to the Danube. Then in 334 B.C.E. Alexander crossed the Hellespont into Asia Minor, which had been controlled by the Persians for over two centuries. With him he brought his army, usually estimated at 30,000 foot soldiers and 5,000 cavalry. It included archers and javelin throwers, used initially to soften up his enemy; cavalry, employed as the primary strike force; infantry phalanxes arranged in block formation with fifteen to eighteen foot spears and shields, utilized to break the back of the enemy resistance; and finally, an elite corps of hypaspists or royal guards, charged with delivering the final blow.

Soon after his crossing Alexander engaged and defeated a numerically superior force at Granicus, opening the door to control of the coastline from the Hellespont to Halicarnassus. By rewarding those cities welcoming him and severely punishing those resisting, Alexander brought the entire western coast of Asia Minor and much of its interior under his control by the spring of 333. Ephesus, Priene, Miletus, Halicarnassus, and Phaselis, all coastal cities, toppled like dominoes. Alexander then led his army southeast approximately two hundred miles, striking inland from Perga to secure the hinterlands. At Gordius, deep in the interior near Ancyra (modern Ankara), Alexander took a sword to the knot (hence *Gordian knot*) which according to legend entitled him to rule Asia.[4]

Leaving Gordius, Alexander marched through Ancyra, turning south to the Mediterranean through Issus down the eastern coast. To his horror, he learned that Darius had sliced in behind him with a large Persian force, butchered his wounded left at Issus, and blocked his line of communication and supply from Macedonia. Alexander had no choice but to stand and fight, and to do so on a spot chosen by the enemy. In the fall of 333 the two armies met at Issus. Pinched between the mountains and the sea, Darius lost the advantage his superior numbers afforded him and Alexander's army was able to rout his forces, putting Darius himself to flight and capturing his family.

Instead of pursuing Darius to the east, however, Alexander surprisingly followed the coast to the south. Most of the cities along the way threw open their gates to him except for Tyre and Gaza. And thus, when the stubborn resistance of Tyre was broken after a seven-month siege, Alexander executed all surviving males and enslaved all women and children. Gaza held out for only two months, enduring a similar fate when it fell.

With this resistance out of the way Alexander set out for Egypt where a people glad for the prospect of relief from Persian tyranny gave him an enthusiastic reception. While wintering his troops in warm, sunny Egypt in 332–331, Alexander explored the land. He sailed the Nile to Memphis, returning to the Mediterranean to the place where he founded the city of Alexandria. Finally he sought an oracle from the god Amon at Siwah, an oasis in the Libyan desert. About that mystery-shrouded visit Arrian says vaguely only that "he received the answer his heart desired."[5]

With control of the coast from Greece to Egypt now in his hands, Alexander deprived the Persian navy of the harbors needed for their replenishment and repair. This daring strategy was evident already in Asia Minor when Alexander dismissed his small fleet rather than risk it against the well equipped, much larger Persian navy. Although his strategy was bold, it owed its success in part to a stroke of good luck. Memnon, the brilliant admiral of the Persian fleet, died quite unexpectedly in 333, and without the logistical support of the ports and its gifted leader the Persian navy was impotent.

On the 14th of November, 332, Alexander became Pharaoh of Egypt. Because of the centrality of the Pharaoh to Egyptian mythology the implications of Alexander's coronation were momentous. Historically in Egypt the Pharaoh was seen as the very god incarnate (i.e., Horus) rather than a mere representative of the god. A complex Egyptian mythology had celebrated the divinity of the king for almost two millennia before Alexander. Thus were the pyramids built as tombs for the pharaohs to provide eternal witnesses to the king's immortality. When Alexander became their king it was natural for the Egyptians to praise him as god.

How seriously Alexander took such gestures, however, or how fully he understood their symbolism is uncertain. Later he did attempt to require the Persian practice of prostration before the king (*proskynesis*) and urged Greek cities to confer divine honors on him, but we cannot know Alexander's mind on this matter. Although for the Persians *proskynesis* was nothing more than a respectful act, the Greeks believed one bent the knee only before a god. Understandably, Alexander's attempt to introduce *proskynesis* angered the Greeks. When Callisthenes refused to bow and laughed contemptuously at Alexander's refusal to kiss him (also an oriental custom), the practice was dropped.

In 331 Alexander again turned his attention to Darius, who after the battle of Issus had limped back to his own capital city of Babylon. First Darius offered generous terms to Alexander. For the return of his family and the cessation of hostilities Darius promised 10,000 talents of gold (an Attic talent weighed 57.85 pounds average), a daughter in marriage, and all of the territory west of the Euphrates. After the overture was crudely rejected by Alexander, Darius raised and trained an army for an unavoidable showdown.

On the 30th of September, 331, Alexander and Darius met once more at Gaugamela, near the Tigris River in modern Iran. Outnumbered in cavalry ten to one, according to one source, Alexander prevailed by arranging his troops in box fashion to frustrate the flanking action of the Persian cavalry. When a crack opened momentarily in the Persian line, Alexander charged with his cavalry straight for Darius, and when the cowardly Darius broke and fled the leaderless and confused Persian force was crushed. Alexander next moved swiftly to occupy Babylon before its rich treasury could be plundered. Then after a month he moved on to Susa, emptied its coffers also, and struck out to claim Persepolis, 400 miles to the southeast. In all, 180,000 talents of gold were taken, a hoard two centuries in the making.

From Persepolis Alexander once more went after Darius. The craven king first fled to his summer capital at Ecbatana in the mountains, then east, seeking refuge with the Bactrians. Alexander's intelligence located Darius at Rhagae, 200 miles to the east of Ecbatana. In forced march he covered the distance with cavalry and infantry(!) in eleven days, but Darius had just left. Alexander rested his troops, then set out for the Caspian Gates, a high mountain pass 45 miles away. After one day of hard marching he camped near the Gates, crossed the pass, selected a small strike force, and made a furious dash across the desert. After 200 miles of rough riding Alexander found Darius fatally stabbed and dumped near Shahrud. Bessus, Darius' Bactrian ally, had executed the Persian king and abandoned his body to allow time for his own escape.

Calling off the pursuit of Bessus, Alexander ordered a funeral for Darius in Persepolis and his burial in the king's tomb. After securing his lines of communication to the rear, he rounded up Darius' Greek mercenaries south of the Caspian sea, accepting the surrender of a number of Persian leaders and installing some as satraps or rulers over Persian provinces. Now east through Parthia, south through Drangiana, and northeast in deep snow through the Hindu Kush, Alexander pursued Darius' murderer.

In Drangiana the first signs of rebellion in the ranks surfaced. Philotas, the commander of the Companions, or cavalry, who knew of a plot against Alexander but failed to report it, was tried before the army, convicted of conspiracy, and executed. His father Parmenion, an able and loyal commander under Philip, was subsequently put to death because he was a popular general in a key position and Alexander wanted to avoid any possibility of a retributive insurgence on account of Philotas. As Arrian put it, "Parmenion was already a grave danger, if he survived when his own son had been put to death, being so highly thought of both by Alexander himself and throughout all the army."[6]

Meanwhile, the Sogdians, fearing reprisals from a pursuing Alexander, handed over Bessus, to whom they had promised sanctuary. He was beaten, imprisoned, and eventually executed for his murder of Darius. Then, after subduing the Scythians to the north, Alexander returned to Bactria for the winter to pacify the Hindu Kush before turning east to India in the summer of 327, where he met some of the stiffest resistance of his entire campaign.

Accepting elephants and cavalry from Taxiles, the ruler of the region between the Jhelum and Chenab Rivers, Alexander joined an alliance against Porus, a powerful and proud ruler to the south. In 326 Alexander drew up facing Porus who was bivouacked on the opposite bank of the Jhelum River (see map). Under cover of darkness Alexander slipped the bulk of his troops across the river upstream and surprised and defeated a stubborn foe. So impressed was Alexander in fact with the tenacity and courage of Porus that he made him ruler of the area. Alexander intended to press on, but his troops, battle-weary and frustrated by the monsoon rains, mutinied, and he had no choice but to turn back.

After collecting a fleet, Alexander set out down the Jhelum to the Indus River and thence to the Indian Ocean brutally and senselessly slaughtering as he went. At Malli Alexander was wounded, almost fatally, when in a foolhardy gesture he led his balking troops over the wall into the city. Downriver near modern Shikarpore Alexander dispatched Craterus with the sick, the wounded and disabled, the elephants, and the baggage train via Arachosia and Carmania. He ordered Nearchus and the fleet to follow the coast.

Meanwhile, Alexander with a large band kept to the coast on foot to resupply the ships. When the Makran coastal range forced them away from the ocean, they suffered indescribable hardship in their march across the desert. Walking at night to avoid the heat, running short of water, bitten by poisonous snakes, stripped of their baggage by a flash flood in a wadi where they had camped, disoriented by sandstorms, they abandoned their pack animals, horses, the stragglers, and the dead. When finally they struggled back to the sea, only *one in seven* survived. Once again they followed the coastline to rendezvous with Craterus and Nearchus near the strait of Hormuz at the entrance to the Persian Gulf. There Alexander turned northwest via Persepolis to Susa where he linked up once more with the fleet.

In 324 smoldering resentment toward Alexander flared up with blazing fury at Opis near Babylon when he announced his intention to discharge loyal, seasoned veterans hobbled by wounds or weakened by age and to return them to Macedonia with a generous bonus. Convinced that Alexander planned to replace them with Persian youth the Macedonians felt betrayed. Acting as one man they demanded that they *all* be discharged. Alexander reacted swiftly and decisively to assert his control. He arrested and executed the ringleaders of the revolt, secluded himself for two days to give the troops time to reconsider, and, when they held firm, gave the order to staff the Companions and the hypaspists with Persian soldiers.

The resolve of the Macedonians cracked; they begged for reinstatement and received swift assurances of reconciliation from a tearful Alexander. "I make you all my kinsmen," he said, a reference to the "Companions," a corps originally bound by blood ties. At a great feast celebrating the reconciliation, Alexander prayed not for the "brotherhood of man," as the great British scholar Tarn maintains, but for "harmony" between Macedonians and Persians. He arranged a mass marriage between his officers and Persian women, but no support exists for the hypothesis that he hoped for a fusion of the races.

In 324 Alexander withdrew from the sweltering heat of Opis to the cool of Ecbatana, Darius' summer capital. His troops played games, staged musical contests, and held elaborate feasts of eating, drinking, and entertainment in honor of Dionysus. In this festival setting, Hephaestion, Alexander's bosom friend and second in command, literally drank himself to death. Alexander's grief was uncontrollable.[7] In honor of Hephaestion, he ordered all sacred fires extinguished throughout the empire, the construction of an imposing memorial, and the retention of the name, "Hephaestion's regiment," even under its new command.

After a frenzy of campaigning to dull the pain of his comrade's death, Alexander headed toward Babylon, while messengers streamed from the western regions with congratulations for his "victorious" eastern campaign. News also came of divine honors bestowed on him in Greece. Alexander's request for such honors, if made, may have been nothing more than a bid to have his spectacular achievements recognized. Such honors had previously been bestowed by the Greeks on persons performing superhuman feats. Heracles, for example, was immortalized for his heroic acts and suffering. Unlike the Hebrews the Hellenes imposed no impassable barrier between the divine and human spheres. Consequently, a petition by Alexander for divine honors, though unusual, was hardly unique to the Greek experience. Alexander's request need not be attributed to a misguided and arrogant attempt to universalize the Egyptian myth of the divine king. Ironically, Alexander's deification by the Greeks barely preceded his demise. Stricken in Babylon after a great banquet with heavy drinking, Alexander died in the late afternoon of June 10, 323, while still in his thirty-third year.

What can we say about Alexander in retrospect? First, most agree he was a military genius. For eleven years he led his troops over a distance of 20,000 miles. In all of those years fighting under all kinds of conditions he never lost a battle. In four pitched battles on strange terrain against huge numerical odds he used his superbly trained and well-equipped cavalry and infantry with consummate skill. Whether against desert guerrillas in Bactria, an elephant brigade in India, a mountain tribe in Afghanistan, an island fortress in the Mediterranean, or a seemingly impregnable bastion perched atop a mountain in India, he possessed an uncanny flair for tactical innovation that assured his success. His courage, and at times even foolhardiness, coupled with his determination, stamina, resourcefulness, and brilliance earned him the title *Aniketos*—the Invincible One.

The mystique of this indomitable figure was contagious and translated into an intimidating fighting force. Both he and his army displayed a swashbuckling style that made them fearsome. He gave no quarter to the enemy or the elements. He traveled light, struck swiftly, and pursued relentlessly. He campaigned summer *and* winter, an entirely new strategy in Asia. He successfully took his army through some of the wildest country in the world. He struggled and fought in deep snow in mountain passes, he crossed the rugged mountains in Afghanistan twice, marched through scorching desert, and forded raging rivers to attack foes who dared him to cross.

Alexander was forceful and decisive when appropriate, and extraordinarily generous when suitable. He pushed his troops to the breaking point, but asked no more of them than he required of himself. Although at times he drove his charges unmercifully, he usually was wise enough to know when to halt for rest and fun—for games, musical contests, and an orgy of eating and drinking. He won the respect of his force by sharing their hardships as well as their successes. When they had no water he drank none. Like them he bore on his body mute testimony of the ugliness and pain of war. In thirteen years of fighting he was wounded four times: in his first Asian battle (Granicus), a sword sliced through his helmet to the skull; at Issus he was wounded in the thigh; in Malli he took a near fatal arrow in the chest, and in Turkestan he broke his leg. Unquestionably Alexander's mental and physical toughness bought respect and discipline in the ranks as well.

In spite of his military genius and positive personal traits, however, Alexander was flawed. He had a fierce and uncontrollable temper; he was arbitrary, stubborn, and brutal. In a drunken rage he snatched a spear from a guard and murdered Clitus who at Granicus had saved his life by severing an arm poised to strike him. To be sure, the attack was provoked by Clitus' drunken taunts, but Alexander's savage response was inexcusable and his subsequent grief showed that he knew it. Alexander justifiably had the officer, Philotas, tried and executed for knowing of but failing to report a conspiracy, but his summary execution of Philotas' father, the gifted, veteran commander Parmenion, for his son's folly was a crude form of justice. Moreover, he savagely reduced cities which resisted him, such as Thebes and Tyre, and made examples of their citizenry. Lastly, his way out of India was marked by a trail of blood let by acts of senseless and ruthless butchery.

Though deeply resented by those who had campaigned with him from the start, Alexander's accommodations to Persian dress and custom and his plans to integrate Persian men into the army served valuable political purposes. The induction of Persians was necessary because the pool of Macedonian young men was too small to control the vast area which he had overrun. Although Alexander's experimentation with the Persian custom of *proskynesis* looks amateurish if not silly, he was flexible enough to drop it after it prompted the ridicule of Callisthenes. For while Alexander was impulsive and headstrong, he was also ready to experiment and willing to change.

Even if he were an extraordinary military leader, Alexander was not just another general bent on conquest and plunder. His leadership was enlightened and his terms to conquered peoples generous. Characteristically, he lowered taxes and gave cities control over their own internal affairs when they welcomed his rule. He freely used indigenous leadership. He established a uniform currency, explored trade routes by sea, opened avenues of communication and commerce between East and West. Wittingly or not, he cleared away barriers to a lively reciprocal exchange of culture, ideas, religion, social forms, and political institutions between Hellenism and the Eastern traditions.

He established cities, though exactly how many is uncertain (Plutarch's number of seventy is undoubtedly an exaggeration). There is no evidence, however, that Alexander hoped the cities would serve as cells of Hellenism which would civilize the barbarians with Greek literature, music, and art. More likely, he established them as centers of commerce and administration. Whatever his aim, though, Alexander's conquests expanded both eastern and western horizons enormously. On this point Tarn was surely correct. Alexander, he said, "lifted the civilized world out of one groove and set it in another; he started a new epoch; nothing could again be as it had been."[8]

Although Alexander did not linger in Palestine except for the two-month siege of Gaza (Josephus' report of a visit to Jerusalem is fictitious), the impact of his conquest on Palestinian and diaspora Jews was far-reaching. We can best learn the scope of his influence through a survey of the rule of Alexander's successors.

Immediately after his death a fierce internecine struggle broke out among Alexander's generals and political appointees for control of his sprawling empire. The battle of Ipsus in 301 established patterns of regional control remaining for almost two centuries. Ipsus confirmed Ptolemy, the senior commander of the phalanx, in control of Egypt and all of Palestine south of Damascus. (Interestingly, by a clever maneuver his procurement of Alexander's embalmed body for Egypt helped secure his position.) Seleucus, a commander of the elite guards (the hypaspists), grabbed territory from northern Syria east through the old Babylonian empire almost to India. Lysimachus,

Alexander's appointed satrap to Persis, took control of Armenia in northern Mesopotamia and Thrace on the north shore of the Aegean Sea. By 270 most of Asia Minor, Mesopotamia, and the ragged edges of the territory east to India came under the Seleucids—i.e., descendants of Seleucus. Meanwhile Macedonia fell to the Antigonids—i.e., descendants of Antigonus Monopthalmus (the One-eyed) whom Alexander had appointed satrap of Phrygia. Egypt, of course, remained in the hands of the Ptolemies.

The Ptolemaic region was held together naturally by a territorial and cultural homogeneity. The Seleucid empire, at the other extreme, was an artificial creation consisting of many peoples, cultures, and languages fractured by party and regional interests constantly threatening to disintegrate it. Because of its geographical proximity to Greece and its experience historically with a large Greek population, the Seleucid Empire was more hellenized than Egypt was. The difference, however, was a matter of degree, for in the third century when Greece was racked by civil war, depression, famine, and a steady decline of her institutions, masses emigrated to Egypt, especially northern Egypt, as well as to Asia Minor. During this time numerous Greek cities sprang up in both the Seleucid and Ptolemaic areas. Naturally, in those cities the language, customs, and culture of Greece prevailed. Inevitably these settlements influenced and were in turn influenced by the non-Greeks in the area. Moreover, the control of the "state" by Hellenists further strengthened the dominant position of the Greek culture.

Israel too was influenced by these hellenistic trends in spite of its historic resistance to outside influence. Its location on the vital corridor linking Egypt and Asia Minor made it impossible for Israel to insulate herself from the "modernizing" tendencies represented by Hellenism. For over a century that influence on Israel was rather subtle because the control of Palestine and Syria remained under the Ptolemies whose rule was benign. In 200 B.C.E., however, that policy changed when the Seleucids decisively defeated the Ptolemies at Paneas in northern Galilee, taking control of all of Palestine.

At first, the changes under Antiochus III, the Seleucid King, were not perceptibly different from those of the Ptolemies. Antiochus' reckless adventures in Thrace and Macedonia, though, alarmed the Romans, who were newcomers to the power struggle in the eastern Mediterranean, and they reacted forcefully. They drove Antiochus from the mainland, catching up with and thoroughly thrashing him at Magnesia in Asia Minor in 190.

The enormous fiscal penalty Rome imposed on Antiochus exhausted his treasury and sent him scurrying for additional revenues. No source was sacrosanct, whether city receipts or temple treasury. In short order the oppressive Roman levy impinged on Israel as well. Seleucid rulers coveted the considerable hoard collected through the temple tax paid by adult Jewish males worldwide. Seleucus IV, Antiochus' successor, sparked off such a popular protest by his attempt to empty this treasury that he abandoned the plan. Later rulers were more successful. When Seleucus' assassination ended his short reign, Antiochus IV (or as he preferred, Epiphanes—i.e., god manifest) became king, and his reign became Israel's nightmare.

Continuing diplomatic and military pressures from Rome fueled the centrifugal forces threatening to tear the Seleucid Empire apart. Desperate to preserve the territorial integrity of his kingdom, Antiochus Epiphanes saw in Hellenism a force of integration as well as a religious and humane symbol of stability that would counter the strain toward fragmentation.

Hellenistic influence had long grown on Judah's soil, even though its roots were shallow. Before the time of Alexander Greek colonies dotted the western shore of Asia Minor. Alexander's successors had founded at least thirty Greek cities within Palestine itself. And in addition Greeks hired as mercenary soldiers by the Persians had served across the Middle East and inevitably had introduced others to Greek ways. Many Semites found it desirable if not necessary to speak the language of the occupying power, which of course was Greek. Greek institutions were transplanted. Art forms were imitated. Many wealthy urban Jews eagerly sought a Greek education for their young men. *Gymnasia* which introduced students to the Greek myths, literary classics, sports, music, and art were built. Architectural styles popular in Greece were copied. Although the Greek soldiers and merchants were no more evangelists for Hellenism than are ours for Americanism, their presence nevertheless contributed mightily to a rising tide of Hellenism.

With the ascendancy of Antiochus Epiphanes in 175 B.C.E., the trend toward hellenization accelerated throughout the next decade. Even in Jerusalem, the symbolic center of Israel's religion, the Jewish aristocracy embraced hellenistic ways, founding a *gymnasium*, giving their children Greek names, following Greek fashions, and at least tolerating if not practicing the worship of Greek gods. Many priests were avid fans of Greek sports (2 Maccabees 4:14), and some Jews even welcomed Antiochus enthusiastically to Jerusalem with a torchlight parade. To promote this trend toward Hellenism Antiochus installed high priests sympathetic to and supportive of his policies, though in assuming the power to appoint high priests the Seleucids were asserting a right never before exercised, the right to control Israel's soul. Antiochus' complete contempt for Judaism is in fact evident in the way he manipulated the high priestly office. For a handsome bribe he replaced Jason, a sycophant whom he appointed to the high priesthood, with Menelaus, a layman unqualified for the position.

Predictably, Antiochus' policies fanned the smoldering resentment of the pious. Insult heaped on top of injury emboldened more and more of the disenchanted to protest the drift toward Hellenism. More traditional Jews cried in outrage when students at the *gymnasium* adopted the uniform worn by their Greek counterparts. Their dress included a short cloak which, unlike modest, traditional Hebrew attire, bared the legs, freeing them for riding. It was also complemented by a broad-brimmed hat. On parade the young men carried a short spear and a downsized shield in the military fashion of the Greek student.

While the religious toleration of the Jerusalem aristocracy was offensive to many in the cities, resentment ran wild in the countryside. Priests especially resented the religious compromises made by their counterparts in Jerusalem with a "pagan" religion. Civil war threatened to erupt between the supporters and opponents of Antiochus' policy of hellenization.[9] Although originally the conflict was between Jewish parties sympathetic or hostile to the drift toward Hellenism, Antiochus mistook the rebellion of the people against the hellenizers as a revolt against his rule. Frustrated by his failure to "annex" Egypt in 168 and fearful that resistance in Judah would undermine his authority elsewhere, Antiochus released the full fury of his military machine on his opponents in Jerusalem. Second Maccabees 5:14 doubtless exaggerates the number of casualties at 80,000 (40,000 killed and 40,000 enslaved), but certainly the carnage was frightful.

No longer willing to "appease" Israel, Antiochus emptied its treasury to gain ready cash, violated the holy of holies, and intensified his policy of hellenization which now symbolized his authority. In 167 Antiochus further ordered the replacement of the Hebrew cult and Torah observance with hellenistic worship. To enforce his policies, he stationed Syrian troops in the Acra, a citadel northwest of the temple, where they remained as a constant irritant until 141. He issued a decree forbidding observance of the sabbath and the festivals, banned circumcision and sacrifice, made possession of a Torah scroll a capital offense, and instituted a monthly observance of a Dionysian rite to commemorate the king's birthday.

Jewish resistance to Antiochus' policies elicited brutal reprisals and further provocative actions. Second Maccabees tells of "Two women . . . brought in for having circumcised their children. These women were paraded about the city, with their babies hung at their breasts, then hurled . . . down headlong from the wall. Others who had assembled in the caves nearby, to observe the seventh day secretly, were betrayed . . . and . . . all burned together" (6:10–11; see also 1 Maccabees 1:59–64). Antiochus ordered the erection of an altar to Zeus on the temple sacrificial altar and the sacrifice of a pig to Dionysus on it (1 Maccabees 1:41–58; 2 Maccabees 6:3–9).

In 167 an incident at Modein, northwest of Jerusalem half way to the coast, set off a firestorm of reaction to Antiochus' "pacification" program and thrust a priestly family into the position of leadership in the resistance movement. Infuriated that a countryman would cooperate with officials of the

Syrian cult in a hellenistic sacrifice, Mattathias, a country priest, first killed the Jewish "volunteer," then the representatives of the Syrian religion (1 Maccabees 2:23–26). Repudiating those compromising the ancestral religion, Mattathias issued a call for an uncompromising loyalty to Torah and to armed resistance. With his five sons Mattathias fled to the remote wilderness of Judah to garner support and make plans for war. Enjoying broad popular support and being intimately familiar with the countryside, Mattathias and his cadre of the fiercely committed used guerrilla tactics with devastating effectiveness. While Antiochus retained control of the cities, the countryside belonged to the people and their warrior-caste of priests.

This old country priest did not live to see the triumph of his cause. When he died in 166 and was succeeded by his third son, Judas Maccabeus, Israel was still a boiling cauldron. (Maccabeus, of unknown origin, did not stem from the Hebrew *maqqebet*, "hammer.") An even more effective leader than his father, Judas took advantage of the Syrian preoccupation with rebellion in Parthia and surprised and routed Seleucid forces at Samaria, Beth-horon, Emmaus, and Beth-zur. In 164 B.C.E. Judas' "freedom fighters" captured Jerusalem, holding it long enough to purge the temple of its pollution from the Zeus altar. (This cleansing of the temple ever since has been celebrated as Hanukkah on the 25th of Chislev, falling in December.)

Judas' ascendancy, however, was temporary. After Antiochus Epiphanes' death, first Lysias (164–162), then Demetrius I (162–150) vigorously campaigned against Judas' army in response to an appeal for help from the Jewish hellenizers in Jerusalem. In a clever political stroke Antiochus' successors lifted the decree prohibiting the practice of the Jewish cult, attempting to defuse the religious issue and to weaken support for the Maccabees. The war nevertheless dragged on, but on the third try the Syrian forces soundly defeated Judas' warriors at Elasa, northwest of Jerusalem, and also killed Judas himself (1 Maccabees 7:1—9:22).

To Jonathan, the youngest brother, now fell the mantle of leadership (160–143). Skillfully exploiting an internal struggle for control of Syria, Jonathan extracted favors from each of the rivals of Israel. By 152 Jonathan persuaded Syria to appoint him high priest, to confirm him as governor (*meridarch*) and to install him officially as *strategos*, the Judean military governor with broad civilian and military powers.

Ironically, after a decade of fighting the Syrian forces, one of the Maccabean family had now become a Syrian official! As *strategos* Jonathan enjoyed direct access to the Seleucid king. After his appointment in 150, he engineered seven years of prosperity, replenished the treasury, and expanded Judah's territorial claims. This euphoric era, however, came to a chilling end in 143 when the Syrian commander, Trypho, lured Jonathan into Ptolemais promising to transfer the city to him; instead he closed the gates, trapped, and executed him.

Now leadership fell to Simon, the lone surviving brother of the original five. Simon succeeded where the other members of the family had failed—he gained political autonomy for Judah. According to 1 Maccabees 15:5–6 the Syrian king says, "Now I grant you all the taxes which the kings before me remitted and all other payments which they remitted. And I have given you the right to mint your own stamped coinage in your country."

With the tribute revoked, subjection to Syria ended. To quote 1 Maccabees again, "the yoke of the Gentiles was removed from Israel" (13:43). The Maccabean family, however, not only won their struggle for religious liberty and political autonomy, they also founded a dynasty which controlled Judah until the Roman subjugation in 63 B.C.E. The Hasmoneans, as they were known (from Hasmon, a family patriarch), had dreams of expansion. With the decline of Syria they widened Judah's territory to the north to include Galilee, west to the coast to embrace the Philistine plain, and extended the borders to the south and the east as well. Not since the time of David had Israel held so much territory.

Ironically, the Maccabean victory over the Seleucids and the extension of her borders did not eradicate hellenistic influence. In fact, under the late Hasmoneans, John Hyrcanus (134–105) and Alexander Janneus (103–76), Hellenism prospered in Israel. Double names, one Hebrew, another Greek were common (note Alexander[!] Janneus). Hellenistic models of kingship and opulent patterns of courtlife were enthusiastically adopted in Israel. Coins were minted with Greek inscriptions as well as Hebrew. Architectural styles again followed hellenistic trends. In Jerusalem, theaters, *gymnasia*, amphitheaters, and such arose once again in the hellenistic mode.

The army of the Hasmoneans followed the Greek model of organization also, and on occasion Greek speaking mercenaries from Pisidia and Cilicia bore arms for the Seleucids. Official proclamations took their form from hellenistic examples and the literature of the period freely copied themes of Greek writings (e.g., the martyrdom of Eliezer in 3 Maccabees clearly appropriates the tradition of Socrates' death). Even under the Romans after 63, hellenistic influence continued unabated. Greek cities razed by the Hasmoneans to avenge past wrongs were rebuilt by the Romans. Patterns established under hellenistic imperialism alone were left in place. So, although Judah broke free from the grip of the Seleucids, even in the Roman period the cultural influence of Hellenism remained.

Yet the Maccabean revolt was no waste. Israel gained her independence in the name of religious devotion. Whatever compromises she made with Hellenism in achieving this result, she had pledged anew her devotion to the one God, Yahweh, and her success in securing that pledge through revolution was permanently etched on her memory. That memory continued as a source of hope and inspiration, later to be invoked in her struggle against Rome.

The Roman Occupation

After its occupation in 63 B.C.E., Rome made all of Palestine a part of the province of Syria and made Hyrcanus II, the last of the Hasmoneans, ruler of Judah in the south. Antipater, an Idumean (a semitic people to the south forced into Judaism by the Hasmoneans), so ingratiated himself with the Romans through his service under Hyrcanus II that he was appointed procurator when Hyrcanus II was slain in 55. Although Judah had lost her autonomy under Rome, her leaders, using skill and imagination, were still able to manipulate the system to secure maximum advantages from Rome.

When Caesar's troops were under a desperate siege in early 47 in Alexandria, Egypt, short of water and outmanned, Antipater rushed to the rescue breaking the blockade with his troops. In gratitude Caesar granted generous privileges to Antipater and his people. He made Antipater a Roman citizen, reduced taxes, gave permission to rebuild the walls of Jerusalem, restored Joppa and a number of towns in the valley of Jezreel to Judah, and extended religious freedom. Since succeeding rulers simply extended these privileges bestowed by Caesar, Antipater's heroic action had enduring significance.

Julius Caesar's assassination in 44 B.C.E. was followed by Antipater's demise by poisoning in 43. These two momentous events timed so closely together triggered a frenetic struggle for control of Judah as well as Rome. Immediately after Antipater's assassination, the Hasmoneans took advantage of the confusion in Rome to reassert their claim to the throne. Antipater's son, Herod, contested the Hasmonean coup, but initially was at a disadvantage. From the very brink of defeat, however, Herod escaped and through some skillful political maneuvering gained confirmation as king of Judea by the Roman senate in 40. By 37 Herod had wrested control from Aristobolus, the Hasmonean representative, whom he ordered first crucified then beheaded. According to Josephus, Herod also executed forty-five Sadducean priests who had supported Aristobolus.

At work in this successful bid for power we see the uncanny political instinct for survival which served Herod throughout his life. In the treacherous waters of Roman power politics where many met their end, Herod not only survived but prospered. After Julius Caesar was slain he first supported Cassius; when this man was defeated, Herod pledged loyalty to Mark Antony; and after Mark Antony's defeat at Actium in 31 he devoted himself to the service of Octavian. This political agility kept him in power over three decades (37–4 B.C.E.) and accounted at least in part for his considerable achievements.

Herod's ability to finesse his way into a winning situation with the Romans, however, secured for him no advantage with the Jews. He was widely hated by the Hebrew people for his mixed ancestry, ruthlessness, imposition of heavy burdens, and collaboration with the Romans. Critics claimed it was safer to be Herod's pig than his son. As an unclean animal, the pig was of no use to Herod, posed no threat to him, and therefore could wander freely unharmed. But because of his paranoia Herod arbitrarily exiled or executed those of his sons whom he suspected of plots against him, liquidated aides who came under suspicion, and sent the woman whom he most deeply loved to her death.

In spite of his demonic nature Herod's long rule benefited Israel in a number of ways. His ambitious construction projects provided employment for thousands. His firm hand as king brought a generation of stability. He led his army in battle on the side of the Romans; dedicated cities to the Emperors, such as Caesarea Maritima, Tiberias, and Celeste; delivered the tax levy on time; and was totally reliable as an ally. Such loyalty elicited favors from Rome beneficial to Israel, even though these were bought at a fearsome price.

After Herod's death in 4 B.C.E., Augustus Caesar divided Israel into three parts, to be ruled by Herod's three sons. In Josephus' words, "he gave half the kingdom to Archelaus with the title of ethnarch [i.e., ruler of a people] and the promise that he should be king if he showed that he deserved it; the other half he divided into two tetrarchies [each a fourth part of the whole] which he bestowed on two other sons of Herod, one on Philip, the other on Antipas" (*The Jewish War* 2:94).[10] Galilee and Perea in the north went to Antipas (4 B.C.E.—39 C.E.), while the region north and east of the Jordan (i.e., Batanaea, Trachonitis, Auranitis as well as some territory around Paneas in northern Galilee) fell to Philip (4 B.C.E.—34 C.E.). The lion's share, however, (Judea, Samaria, and cities on the plain from Gaza to Joppa) came under Archelaus, the least able of the three.

Because of his brutality and incompetence, Archelaus stood trial and lost his kingdom in 6 C.E. He was replaced by a Roman procurator. Except for one short period, from 41–44 C.E. under Herod Agrippa, Judah remained under the administration of a Roman procurator continuously from 6–66 C.E. Rome also appointed the high priests as had the Seleucids and gave custody of the high priestly vestments to the procurator. While Rome allowed Israel freedom of worship and religious practice, it infringed on those privileges often enough to cause deep-seated uneasiness among the Jews.

Because the land in the hill country was marginally productive and rainfall unpredictable, the Roman taxes were burdensome. Drought or insects often drove the small farmer into indentured service to larger landlords, caused him to forfeit his property, and often forced him in desperation to turn to robbery for survival. Indignation festered against rich landlords, tax collectors, and Roman administrators. The times were ripe for prophetic figures promising divine deliverance from the heavy burdens, or even for revolutionary leaders who dreamed of liberating Judah from the Roman rule.

Josephus tells of sporadic Jewish resistance from as early as 6 C.E., when Judas the Galilean unsuccessfully opposed the Roman census. Judas, according to Josephus, incited his countrymen to revolt, upbraiding them as cowards for consenting to pay tribute to the Romans and tolerating mortal masters, after having God for their Lord (*War* 2:118). Such active resistance to Roman occupation is best understood in light of the earlier, successful revolt of the Maccabees against hellenistic imperialism in 167–142 B.C.E.

Armed with the memory of the Maccabean success many believed God would reward their resistance to a superior Roman force with a miraculous intervention assuring victory and liberty. Judas, however, did not achieve the hoped for liberation, but in the decades following Judas a number of humiliating episodes added to the store of hatred making the situation even more volatile. Though resistance was intermittent and mostly passive in the first half of the century, a reservoir of rage accumulated which broke loose in a torrent of violence in 66 C.E.

One person who contributed considerably to this rising tide of resentment was Pontius Pilate. Under the cover of darkness Pilate, the procurator from 26–36 C.E. whom the gospels link with Jesus' trial, sneaked Roman troops into Jerusalem bearing standards inscribed with Roman images. Pilate's senseless act was a blatant violation of the first commandment banning the manufacture or worship of any graven image. Deeply offended Jews caused such an uproar that Pilate withdrew his troops. When they trailed him to Caesarea and staged a sit-in protesting this blasphemy, Pilate threatened reprisals unless they dispersed. Unfazed, they forced his hand by offering their necks to his sword and Pilate relented. As Josephus puts it, "they were ready to die rather than transgress the Law" (*War* 2:174).

Although the resistance was passive it reflected the depth of anger at Pilate's sacrilege. Pilate later humiliated the Jews when he seized funds from the temple treasury (*War* 2:175–177). Taking the Jewish protest as provocation Pilate acted decisively, killing some Jews and imprisoning others. Finally, in 36 C.E. Pilate was recalled to Rome after ordering an attack on a group of unarmed Samaritans on a pilgrimage to Mt. Gerizim.

The reader will recall the role in which Pilate is cast in the four Gospels. When Jesus is brought before Pilate for trial, in one Gospel Pilate after perfunctory questioning finds Jesus innocent but accedes to the crowds' demand to "crucify him" (Mark 15:1–15). Both Matthew and Luke, however, exon-

erate Pilate shifting the blame to "the Jews" (Matt. 27:1–2; 11–26; Luke 23:1–
12). In John, Pilate's role in the affair is open to interpretation (John 18:28—
19:16). Although Matthew, Luke, and John refashion the Pilate episode to
serve later theological interests, there is no question in these three accounts
that Pilate actively participated in the trial and that Jesus met his death at the
hands of the procurator's guard.

Pilate had good reason to "wonder" about Jesus. He came preaching the
"kingdom of God is at hand." Pilate had enough experience with Jewish
resistance to know that the kingdom was no spiritualized concept. The gospel
of the kingdom would naturally gather unto itself the hopes and expectations
of an oppressed people. Any proclamation of a kingdom presumes a rival
claimant, a king. With justification Pilate asked, "Are you the king of the
Jews?" The gospel tradition offers no opinion on Pilate's competence; only
his participation in the proceeding is noted. But the trial of Jesus before Pilate
reflects the nervousness of the Romans about resistance movements.

In 37–41 C.E. the Emperor Gaius arbitrarily suspended the traditional
religious privileges accorded to Jews and sought to introduce the Imperial
Cult, or worship of the Emperor, into the temple itself. Jews massed at Tiberias in Galilee and on the Plain of Ptolemais to protest his plan. They
threatened to leave the fields untilled, depriving Rome of its tribute, and if
necessary to "sacrifice the entire Jewish nation" to frustrate Gaius' plan (*War*
2:197). Violence was barely averted when King Agrippa interceded and the
order was cancelled.

Philo's *The Embassy to Gaius* gives independent confirmation of Gaius'
madness. Philo led the embassy in protest against a massacre of Jews for
stubbornly resisting the order of the Roman prefect, Flaccus, who ordered
all Jews to pay homage to images of Gaius. Leading the embassy to Gaius
was risky, but Philo handled the appeal so skillfully that further reprisals from
Gaius were avoided and eventually the Jews secured protection from mali-
cious looting and mob violence.

When Fadus was procurator (44–46 C.E.), a prophet named Theudas
attempted to lead a band of Jews across the Jordan, perhaps drawing from the
memory of God's intervention to rescue Israel from Egyptian bondage. This
group, engaged in no more than a symbolic gesture of liberation, was probably relatively small and unarmed. Yet it was intercepted by Roman troops
and Theudas and many of his disciples were slaughtered. Until this incident
Jewish resistance was largely passive; from this time on, however, a series of
incidents provoked increasingly violent Jewish reaction.[11] Josephus refers to
an obscene gesture made by a Roman soldier from the roof of the temple
portico at Jews gathered below for a sacred feast (*War* 2:224). Tempers flared,
pilgrims pelted the soldiers with rocks, the troops overreacted, and several
Jews died in a flight of panic.

In 51 C.E. after an especially explosive incident occurred between Jews and Samaritans, who were bitter rivals, the Roman procurator, Cumanus, first temporized until the strife turned ugly, then sided with the Samaritans against the poorly armed Jewish resisters. Again many Jews died and scores were imprisoned. Although Cumanus was removed from office for incompetence, the damage was done and its effects lingered, festering like a sore.

From 51 C.E. on, then, violent Jewish resistance flared with increasing frequency. The Sicarii (from *sicae*, daggers concealed under their clothing) turned more and more to acts of terrorism. Coming mainly from the rural lower classes they assassinated Jews who collaborated with the Romans; they kidnapped officials and held them hostage to secure the release of imprisoned Sicarii; they robbed to secure funds for arms and food. As Josephus tells it,

> [they] committed murders in broad daylight in the heart of the city. The festivals were their special seasons, when they would mingle with the crowd, carrying short daggers concealed under their clothing, with which they stabbed their enemies. Then, when they fell, the murderers joined in the cries of indignation and, through this plausible behaviour, were never discovered. The first to be assassinated by them was Jonathan the high priest; after his death there were numerous daily murders (*War* 2:254–56).

The Sicarii considered the Roman occupation to be godless. They therefore believed their cause was just and that with God's help they would purge the land and restore the sanctity of Israel. In the period before the war the Sicarii sowed confusion and anarchy both in the countryside and in Jerusalem. At the beginning of the war they joined the Zealot struggle in Jerusalem.[12] After a brief period, however, they withdrew to Masada, a Herodian stronghold on the Dead Sea, and there they remained until the final siege of the Roman Tenth Legion in 74 C.E.[13] With conscripted Jewish laborers, the Tenth Legion built a dirt ramp to the top of the stronghold, moved their battering rams into position, and began their relentless pounding. Once they breached the outer wall the Sicarii committed mass suicide rather than surrender. Only two women with five small children survived by hiding in the underground water conduits.

Under the procurator Florus (64–66 C.E.) the situation degenerated even further. When Jews protested his illicit appropriation of seventeen talents from the temple treasury, Florus released troops to sack, plunder, and massacre innocent and helpless people (*War* 2:293–308). Priests from the lower ranks responded by refusing to accept gifts or sacrifices from any foreigners for temple service. Thus, in effect, the priests repudiated the custom of offering sacrifices daily on behalf of the Roman emperor and the empire. This action was a clear violation of an agreement between the Romans and Jews which exempted Jews from practicing the state religion in exchange for a daily sacrifice for the emperor. Sacrifice symbolized Jewish loyalty to the empire but not worship of the emperor; consequently, the Romans viewed the unilateral suspension of the agreement as an act of war. When the chief priests and Pharisees were unable to reverse this interpretation, war broke out.

After an internal struggle the city fell into the hands of the Zealots who sought unsuccessfully to defend it against the Romans. The ranks of the Zealots were drawn from lower class priests, some "brigands" from the countryside and dissident elements within the city who were intent on overthrowing the aristocratic, provisional, Jewish government which ruled at the pleasure of the Romans. The counsel of moderation offered by the Pharisees and Sadducees was repudiated (see discussion below). The Zealots were determined to purge Israel of all defilement contracted by association with the Romans. Their aim was to gain freedom from foreign domination, taxes, and even from sacrifices and prayer on behalf of the Roman emperor.

Rome was determined to quench the fires of revolution in Israel. After a disastrous and half-hearted attempt to take Jerusalem in 66 C.E., Cestus Gallus withdrew, perhaps because he was unprepared to spend the winter in the siege, and took 6,000 casualties in retreat. Upon hearing of the reverse, Nero dispatched a seasoned veteran, Vespasian, and his son, Titus, to put down the revolt. It took most of 67 C.E. to pacify Galilee. Vespasian lost valuable time waiting all of 68 for orders which never came from Rome. In 69 Vespasian became Emperor. Thus, not until 70 was the siege begun in earnest under Titus with four full legions (perhaps as many as 60,000 troops). Meanwhile civil strife raged within Jerusalem as Zealots, Sicarii, and moderates struggled for power. Attacking from the north, one wall of defense after another fell to the Roman battering rams. In August the Roman troops broke through. They sacked and burned the city. They rooted out the last resisters from the temple and put the torch to it. Israel's most holy shrine, standing since the return from Babylonian bondage over six hundred years before, was reduced to ashes and rubble in a few short hours.

Josephus tells how the soldiers torched the temple, looted, and ruthlessly butchered both children and the aged, killing indiscriminately both those begging mercy and those resisting. The roar of the flames was periodically broken by the groans of the fallen. Josephus adds,

> Such were the height of the hill and the vastness of the blazing edifice [i.e., the temple] that the entire city seemed to be on fire, while as for the noise, nothing could be imagined more shattering or more horrifying. There was the war-cry of the Roman Legions as they converged; the yells of the partisans encircled with fire and sword; the panic flight into the arms of the enemy of the people cut off above; their shrieks, as the end approached (War 6:277; [Williamson]).

We gain faint glimpses of that terror in those last hours now from the archeological data. Recently archeologists unearthed a comfortable six-room house and bath in the old city that gave mute but poignant testimony of the final siege in 70 C.E. As the Roman army devastated the city, plundering as it went, the house of the bar Kathros family was reduced to ashes and remained undisturbed until unearthed this century. Most members of the household had fled for their lives, but one young woman was not so fortunate. The bones of her arms were found in the ashes inclining against a wall with one outstretched hand on a step. Her skeleton remains as a silent testimony to the tragic destruction of Jerusalem which left a deep and jagged scar indelibly etched on Israel's soul.[14]

Although the revolt erupted after Jesus' death, he was surely aware of the seething anger against the Romans in the hearts of his countrymen and their contempt for Jews who made easy accommodations with Roman interests. Even though the Gospels were all written after the Jewish–Roman War (with the possible exception of Mark), they all contain allusions to unrest from this prewar period.

All four Gospels recall the political context of the passion. Jesus was tried before a Roman procurator—"suffered under Pontius Pilate"—and on suspicion of political crimes was executed in the Roman fashion by the procurator's guard. The insistance of the Gospel writers that Jesus was innocent of the charge for which he was punished hardly presumes that his message was apolitical. The theological talk placed on Jesus' lips had clear political overtones in this setting, just as the political statements were always couched in theological terms. It is inappropriate, therefore, to impose a discrete separation such as we seek to maintain between church and state on the first-century setting.

To a first-century Jew any credible announcement of the imminent arrival of the kingdom of God would have been electrifying, for to them the kingdom was no mere spiritualized concept. The Jewish tradition was suffused with stories celebrating Yahweh's kingship and his triumph over Israel's foes. From the time of the Seleucid persecution the people recalled Daniel's prediction of God's victory over Israel's oppressors and his establishment of an everlasting kingdom for the righteous (Dan. 6:26; 7:14, et al.). The Qumran community eagerly awaited God's war of liberation against all the "sons of perdition."[15] The Psalms of Solomon celebrate Yahweh's kingship over Israel's foes (ch. 17).[16] Prophets arose periodically in the spirit and power of Yahweh, raising hopes of a victory over the Romans like that of the Maccabees over the Seleucids. Consequently Jesus' proclamation, "The kingdom of God is at hand," inevitably would evoke a set of images which carried powerful political associations for many. Titles like "king" or "son of David," when applied to a messianic figure, only intensified those expectations.

Although the symbol "kingdom of God" contained a rich store of associations for the Jewish people, the Gospel writers gave the term fresh applications. Jesus' friendship with sinners, tax collectors, the impious, the ritually unclean, the poor, prostitutes, and with the dispossessed and disenfranchised in society reversed traditional expectations. The kingdom envisioned by Jesus gave priority to the powerless and those without status or current rewards. Those then in power—the Herodians, Scribes, Priests, Sadducees, et al.— could hardly expect to retain their positions of privilege and influence in the coming kingdom. We see, therefore, how even Jesus' inclusion of those on the fringes of power, without status or recognition, carried distinct political overtones.

Since the Gospels were all written a generation or more after Jesus' death, some fresh interpretation was dictated by the needs of each writer's audience. Necessarily the Gospel writers had to reinterpret the highly charged political image of Jesus which they inherited. The political realities of their own time also required some shift of emphasis. Luke, for example, may insist on the innocence of Paul in his Acts to counter charges of disloyalty to the Empire raised against Christians. Both Matthew and Luke shift blame away from Pilate onto the Jews for the crucifixion of Jesus. Mark's Gospel underscores the confession of the Roman soldier at the cross, "Surely this man was a son of God." Jesus' response to the question, "Is it lawful to pay taxes to Caesar or not?" has continuing relevance for a church that wishes to avoid the charge of disloyalty to the Empire. We see, therefore, how both these traditions, which can be reliably assigned to Jesus and the interpretation of the Gospel writers, associate theological affirmations with the dominant political realities of the day.

Paul, writing before the war, likewise sees correlations between the gospel he preaches and political structures. Although they are transitional—"the forms of this world are passing away"—they are nevertheless important. Where a rampant religious enthusiasm might lead some to disassociate themselves from the social and political structures, Paul urged believers to pay their taxes and to honor the governing authorities. Paul felt that the state as a servant of God (Rom. 13:4,6) protected the human community from the terrors of anarchy by rewarding good and punishing evil. And although he believed the end was near (Rom. 13:11–13), the lateness of the hour did not cancel civic duty; it gave it cosmic significance.

Paul believed the state was useful in temporarily providing an ordered society in which travel and witness could go unhindered. Thus although the believer's allegiance was to the new order, there was still the need to serve the present provisional order. All such discussion by Paul was political talk couched in theological language. One is entitled to wonder if Paul would have said the same thing had he lived to see the persecutions under Nero and Domitian. Would he then have been able to call the state a "servant of

God," or would he have agreed with the author of Revelation that the state was a "monster"?

Elsewhere we read the signature that the Jewish–Roman War left on the New Testament. It seems clear that after the war tensions increased between Jews and Christians. We learn from Paul's letters that before the conflict it had been possible to hold Jesus as the Messiah and still share in synagogue life. Afterward, however, this relationship was strained. By the time of Matthew's Gospel the arguments were shrill and acrimonious (around 85 C.E.), and the fourth Gospel assumes that confessing Jesus as Messiah would have meant expulsion from the synagogue. In Matthew's Gospel the destruction of the temple in 70 C.E. was interpreted as punishment for the rejection of Jesus by most Jews.

Because pacifistic Jewish Christians apparently refused to support the revolution they naturally would be seen as either cowards or traitors. Gentile Christians might have sought to avoid Roman reprisals by disassociating themselves from the nationalistic cause of the Zealots. This disassociation ultimately led not only to a rupture between the synagogue and the church but also between Jewish and Gentile Christians. We see, therefore, that political forces played an important role in framing the context of Jewish messianism, and profoundly influenced the proclamation of Jesus, the development of the early church, and the shaping of the New Testament.

Chapter 2

Forms of Religious Expression

The New Testament refers to various clusters of first-century religious expression almost casually. We are told that Paul was a Pharisee, that Jesus was crucified between two bandits, that John the Baptist baptized for the forgiveness of sins like the Essenes at Qumran, that the Jesus of the Gospels encountered Sadducees, priests, scribes, and Levites, and that he freely socialized with the "people of the land" (*'am ha-'aretz*), sinners, tax collectors, the poor, the sick, the troubled.

This broad spectrum of Jewish piety informed the Christian *kerygma* (or proclamation) and provided the milieu in which the early church was rooted. Christianity was in the beginning a Jewish sect, after all, sharing but reinterpreting the hallowed precepts of Judaism. The church's messianism owed its own genesis to traditional Jewish hopes and expectations, but the proclamation that Jesus of Nazareth was *the* Messiah challenged long-existing symbol systems and provoked sharp clashes with established religious factions. Awareness of this group's debt to the Hebrew tradition and of their manner of departure from the religious conventions of the day will help us appreciate both the distinctiveness of the church's *kerygma* and the reasons for both its polemical tendencies and its appeal for Jews and Gentiles alike.

No portion of the Mediterranean world, including Palestine, was devoid of hellenistic influence. Moreover, the expansion of the church and the writings of that community reflect an ongoing dialogue with the hellenistic world. Hellenistic piety influenced many recipients of Paul's letters, and the vocabulary and outlook of this worldview are a part and parcel of the leavening process evident in the writings themselves. Thus, in the discussion below we shall look at both Jewish and hellenistic forms of religious expression, for both together are a part of the context in which the New Testament's lively dialogue is intimately engaged.

Forms of Jewish Religious Expression

The Pharisees

The religious group most frequently mentioned in the New Testament is the Pharisees, and references to them are mixed. In Acts Luke speaks positively of Paul's Pharisaism. Going beyond what Paul reports in his letters, Luke suggests that the Apostle even remained a loyal Pharisee to the end. Furthermore, in Acts 5:34–39, Gamaliel, the Pharisee, argued for tolerance of the Christian sect within Judaism, and in 15:5 we are told a number of Pharisees were Christians. Paul discounts his considerable achievements as a Pharisee as "refuse" for the sake of the gospel; yet this statement should not be taken as a repudiation of his past, but as a revaluation of it in light of his belief in the messianic Jesus. In Philippians 3:5,6 the Apostle refers to himself as "circumcised on the eighth day, of the people of Israel, of the tribe of Benjamin, a Hebrew born of the Hebrews; as to the law a *Pharisee* . . . as to righteousness under the law blameless" (emphasis added). But even where Paul does not explicitly mention his Pharisaism, its continuing influence on him, as we shall see later, is evident.

While some references to the Pharisees in Luke's Gospel are negative, positive allusions occur also. In 13:31, for instance, the Pharisees seek to warn Jesus of Herod's plan to kill him. But Luke's sometimes positive assessment differs dramatically with the almost uniformly unflattering treatment of the Pharisees in the Gospel of Matthew. Although they possess some redeeming qualities—they seek baptism (3:7) and fast (9:14), for instance—Matthew generally maligns the Pharisees in harshly negative terms. They appear as "vipers" (3:7; 12:34; 23:33), "hypocrites" (23:23,27), "blind guides" (23:16,24), keepers of the law who neglect "justice and mercy and faith" (23:23), murderers of the prophets (23:31), and "whitewashed tombs" (23:27). In the Gospel of John the picture is equally critical. Nicodemus, a Pharisee, seeks a sign (3:1ff.) and assists in the burial of Jesus (19:39–42), but otherwise the statements about the Pharisees, as in the Gospel of Matthew, are sharply critical, mirroring the struggle between church and synagogue in a later period. They therefore should not be read as objective description. Let's briefly consider some of the findings of scholarly research on first-century Pharisaism then, in order to help us better understand the New Testament's apparently prejudicial representation of this group.

Although this description by the Gospel writers and by Paul distorts historical reality somewhat, much that is historically reliable may nonetheless be learned from these accounts. In the customs of the Pharisees we find a strong emphasis on the observance of laws of purity. Following tradition they would take a ritual bath after returning from the market place, after touching a corpse, or after having certain bodily discharges in order to lift up clean hands in prayer before their meals. They ritualistically cleansed, not merely washed, vessels, cups, and pots used either in food preparation or in consumption (Mark 7:3–4). They excluded "unclean" persons such as tax collectors, the ill, the physically handicapped, or the emotionally disturbed from table fellowship (e.g., Mark 2:16). They fasted (Mark 2:18), tithed "mint and rue and every herb" (Luke 11:42), occupied conspicuous places in the synagogue (Luke 11:43), and rigorously observed sabbath law.

Jacob Neusner holds that, except for fasting, this agenda comports rather well with that of the rabbinic traditions.[1] The Gospels do tend to leave us with the impression that the Pharisees treated all of life as a ritual, and Neusner's studies reveal how important this cultic aspect of Pharisaism really was. Unlike the priests in Leviticus who interpreted the laws concerning sacrifice and the consumption of food offerings as applying *only* to the temple, the Pharisees believed the "setting for law observance was the field and the kitchen, the bed and the street."[2] This sect took seriously if not literally the command in Exodus to become a "kingdom of priests," thus treating all aspects of daily life as if it were a part of the temple service.

As important as was this intense preoccupation with the laws of purity, sabbath observance, the festivals, etc., Pharisaism doubtless embraced other emphases as well. Josephus mentions additional features in the following description:

> . . . the Pharisees, who are considered the most accurate interpreters of the laws, and hold the position of the leading sect, attribute everything to Fate and to God; they hold that to act rightly or otherwise rests, indeed, for the most part with man, but that in each action Fate co-operates. Every soul, they maintain, is imperishable, but the soul of the good alone passes into another body, while the souls of the wicked suffer eternal punishment (*War* 2:162–63).

Proud of his own Pharisaic connection, Josephus tells us that this "leading sect" which was so intent on applying the law to all aspects of life also affirmed a classical paradox—the belief that God fixes human destiny (Fate) and simultaneously requires responsible human behavior. The words of the Mishnah, though late, aptly express this first-century view: "All is foreseen; but freedom of choice is given" (Aboth 3:16). A second-century rabbi, Akiba, held the similar opinion that though all is in the hands of heaven, the human is nevertheless free. Moreover, the value of every soul in Pharisaism was linked with the belief in the resurrection of the righteous which is to occur "at the grand, final assize when God will vindicate his pious people and punish sinners."[3] Unlike the inhospitable Sadducees, the Pharisees, according to Josephus, "are affectionate to each other and cultivate harmonious relations with the community" (*War* 2:166). And, unlike the Essenes, who seek to live in isolation, the Pharisees dwell among townfolk and are intensely involved in the workaday world.

It is unclear if Josephus was unaware of the violent, abusive, and even fatal internecine confrontations between two groups of Pharisees, the Shammaites and Hillelites, or simply chose to ignore them. In his romanticized account, however, Josephus merely says the Pharisees live simply, avoid any pretense of luxury, and, because of the recognition of their strict observance of the religion, are "extremely influential among the townsfolk; and all prayers and sacred rites of divine worship are performed according to their exposition" (*Jewish Antiquities* 18:15).[4]

In their respect for the teachings of the elders we see an openness to tradition and divine instruction which extends beyond the first five books of Hebrew Scriptures, the Pentateuch. Whether that tradition was oral (as Rivkin claims) or not (as Neusner argues) the Pharisees certainly ascribed authority to instruction outside the written Scriptures.[5] They claimed a tradition that was broad and inclusive, embracing the writings (the wisdom materials, the Psalms, etc.), the prophets, and the sayings of the sages. In their openness to sacred traditions beyond the Pentateuch, their belief in the resurrection, which originated perhaps as late as 167 B.C.E., and in their translation of the Levitical code into all aspects of daily life we see a remarkable openness to innovation.

The tendency of earlier scholars like Schuerer, Strack and Billerbeck, Bousset, Bultmann, Conzelmann, Jeremias, and Lohse to accept uncritically the later rabbinic traditions as accurate descriptions of Pharisaism before 70 C.E. is no longer possible. Neusner argues that the concerns which the Gospel writers ascribe to the Pharisees conforms rather well with the emphasis isolated in early strands of the Mishnah, a written collection of Pharisaic traditions that took shape around 200 C.E.[6] While these early traditions conflict somewhat with the description of the Pharisees given by Josephus, this hardly implies that Josephus' observations are unhistorical. It is more likely that there was more diversity in first-century Pharisaism than we as yet acknowledge and that from one period to another the emphasis changed. Thus, the early political involvement of the sect gave way in the first century to a form of piety defined by tithing, fasting, sabbath and festival observance, oaths, keeping the laws of purity, etc.

While Neusner believes that Pharisaism in Jesus' day was quietistic and apolitical, concerned primarily with matters of ritual, Rivkin takes the opposite view—that Pharisaism was revolutionary and concerned with a wide range of issues beyond ritual purity. The Pharisaic concern for the rites of cleanliness, Rivkin claims, was subordinated to Pharisaic concern for the two-fold law (i.e., oral and written) and a strenuous political effort to impose that law on society.[7] Rivkin maintains that the writings of Josephus, rabbinic traditions, the Apocrypha and Pseudepigrapha of the Old Testament, and the New Testament all share a common view: the Pharisees were popular with the masses, served as a scholar class interpreting both oral and written traditions, believed in individual immortality, and promulgated new law.

From the time of the Maccabean revolt on, though, Rivkin thinks the Pharisees were the dominant political and religious force in Israel. Through a quiet revolution they replaced the priests and Jewish aristocracy as interpreters of the law and dictated policy to the Sadducees. Popular with the people and pursuing a moderate course, they accommodated themselves to Roman authority so long as their religious laws were not violated, and even after the revolt of 66–70 C.E. they participated in political negotiations with the Romans.

According to Rivkin the New Testament shares this basic image of Pharisaism as well. Paul, for example, recalls his Pharisaic past (Phil.3:5–6) when he was "so extremely zealous . . . for the traditions of my fathers" (Gal. 1:14). Matthew 23:2 speaks of the Pharisees as those who "sit on Moses' seat"—i.e., serve as authoritative interpreters of the law as a scholar class. Their power and prestige are acknowledged by the recognition they receive in the marketplace, the deference shown to them as "Rabbi," the seats of honor they occupy in the synagogue, the special imperative they have to persecute Christians (Acts 9:1–2). Mark notes their concern with ritual laws of purity (Mark 7:1–13), but also notes the position of authority from which they demand evidence or proofs of the authenticity of Jesus' message (8:11– 13). Other references attest to their belief in life after death and angels (Acts 23:8).

Neusner may be criticized for his narrow, reductionistic view of Pharisaism and Rivkin, for his uncritical reading of Josephus' description of the Pharisees and his tendency to force all other evidence into the pattern outlined by Josephus.[8] Rivkin's homogenization of historical evidence greatly oversimplifies the picture of the Pharisees in the first century. He passes over non-Pharisaic traditions (e.g., Jubilees and the Dead Sea Scrolls) that speak for an oral tradition elsewhere, and erroneously thinks that the Pharisees and the Scribes were one and the same. Yet Rivkin's thesis, as well as Neusner's, does find support in the New Testament. At this point more evidence is needed before agreement can be reached. What both Rivkin and Neusner do establish, however, is that a significant Pharisaic presence is taken for granted in the New Testament.

Although the Gospels contest Pharisaic views even when their debt is manifest, it is in the accounts of and by Paul that Pharisaic influence is most obvious. Paul, you will remember, was a zealous Pharisee before his apostolic call (Phil. 3:5). In the defense which Luke places on the Apostle's lips in Acts 25:8, Paul appears as a loyal Pharisee even while confessing Jesus as the Christ: "Neither against *the law of the Jews,* nor against the temple, nor against Caesar have I offended at all" (emphasis added). Although Luke's account may go too far, Paul, as his letters prove, did share many Pharisaic beliefs even as an Apostle. His anticipation of the resurrection and judgment at the end of the age, the tie he secured between divine predestination and human responsibility, his acceptance of a broad range of traditions as scriptural, his methods of biblical interpretation, and perhaps even some of his intensity can all be traced to his Pharisaic roots.

At other points, however, Paul appears to reject his religious past. He freely consorts with Gentiles, ignores the laws of purity, and interprets the law as provisional, all of which separate him from his Pharisaic brothers. His acceptance of Jesus as Messiah—one who had befriended religious outcasts, was careless of the laws of purity, and had died a cursed death—would also pit Paul against many of the Pharisees. Paul certainly did compromise his Pharisaic tradition, but to suggest that he flatly and decisively repudiated it is going too far. It might be better to say Paul appraised those traditions in a fresh way in light of his understanding of the cross and resurrection of Jesus as God's action in history.[9]

The Sadducees

The New Testament rarely mentions the Sadducees,[10] which hardly does justice to the impact this small "party" had on the Jewish social setting of the first century. Intimately associated with the temple, the most important religious symbol of Jesus' day, the Sadducees were a priestly aristocracy occupying the apex of the social pyramid. It is unlikely that all were actually priests, yet their position in the society was legitimized by their priestly heritage. Their history was rooted, it was thought, in the subsoil of Israel itself. Claiming to come from Zadok, a priest under David, and chief priest under Solomon (2 Sam. 15:27; 20:25; 1 Kings 2:35) their lineage (if their claim is true) preceded that of the temple. Although the genesis of the Saducean "party" can be traced back only to the Maccabean period (167–142 B.C.E.), their authority, wealth, and privilege in first-century Palestine was already legendary. As late as the earlier part of the second century B.C.E. the author of Ecclesiasticus urges his readers to "give thanks unto him that chose the sons of Zadok to be the priests" (51:12). Their lofty position, however, and the compromises necessary to secure it earned them the dislike and even contempt of some groups, as we shall see later.

The description of the Sadducees by Josephus is far from flattering, but that is hardly surprising given his admitted Pharisaic bias. Unlike the Pharisees who showed "affection to one another and cultivate[d] harmonious relations with the community" (*War* 2:166), the Sadducees are, in his opinion, "rather boorish . . . with their peers" and "rude . . . to aliens" (*War* 2:166). Elsewhere Josephus accuses the Sadducees of being elitists who have "the confidence of the wealthy alone but no following among the populace," unlike the Pharisees who "have the support of the masses" (*Antiquities* 13:298).

Although not all Sadducees were priests, the temple worship and administration were under the direction of this small circle. The Sadducees probably occupied the majority of the seats on Israel's highest court, the Sanhedrin, although Pharisees held positions on the court as well. In any case Israel's aristocracy—small, rich, well educated, and powerful—was made up almost entirely of the Sadducees. Bent on retaining their position of influence and privilege, the Sadducees were conservative both religiously and politically. Undeniably, many accommodated themselves to the Roman rule and collaborated with the Romans to implement policies of the Empire that benefited them. Yet is is inaccurate to call the Sadducees sycophants of Roman political interests.

In the last two decades before the War (66–70 C.E.) many influential Sadducees appealed to Rome to reverse decisions of the procurators appointed by Rome. In other cases Sadducees protested the incompetence of Roman officials and were instrumental in securing their removal from office. Other Sadducees were angered by the insensitivity and ineptness of many procurators. Sometimes they defied them, at other times they negotiated with them, and on occasion they even bribed them in order to effect change in the political process. Some of the Sadducees might even be termed courageous, losing their lives in support of moderate policies when moderation was unpopular. Most were political realists who were aware of the might of the Roman army and the capacity of Roman officials for arbitrary action. Through political influence and compromise the majority sought to realize the art of the possible, steering a middle course between collaboration and revolt.

Concerning the beliefs of the Sadducees Josephus suggests that they "hold that only those regulations should be considered valid which were written down (in Scripture), and that those which had been handed down by former generations need not be observed" (*Antiquities* 13:297). However, this passage does not imply, as once was thought, a repudiation of the oral traditions of the fathers cherished by the Pharisees. As we saw above, the prominent position enjoyed by the oral tradition among the Pharisees *may* have come after 70 C.E.

The Sadducees did, however, follow a more conservative interpretation of Scripture than did the Pharisees. Their constructions were literal as far as practicable and they assigned the preeminent place on the scale of scriptural truth to the Pentateuch. The prophets and the writings, though still considered scriptural by them, were assigned a position of secondary importance

(*Antiquities* 13:297). In disputes over the law, the Sadducees vigorously defended their prerogatives as the supreme custodians of scriptural truth and the only accurate interpreters of the law. They opposed all innovation, such as the Pharisaic belief in the resurrection, and, according to Josephus, they offered a stricter, even harsh application of the law: they "are indeed more heartless than any of the other Jews . . . when they sit in judgment" (*Antiquities* 20:199).

Josephus contrasts the Pharisees with the Sadducees, who "do away with Fate altogether. . . . They maintain that man has the free choice of good or evil, and that it rests with each man's will whether he follows the one or the other. As for the persistence of the soul after death, penalties in the underworld, and rewards, they will have none of them" (*War* 2:165). Elsewhere Josephus notes that the "Sadducees hold that the soul perishes along with the body" (*Antiquities* 18:16). The sketch Josephus draws of the Sadducees is undoubtedly distorted, yet the impressions he leaves approximate those mentioned in the New Testament.

In Acts 23:8, for example, we learn that "the Sadducees say there is no resurrection, nor angel nor spirit." Mark 12:18–27 tells of a question the Sadducees raised to show how ridiculous the belief in the resurrection was. According to the Levirate law from Deuteronomy 25:5–10, surviving brothers were obligated to marry the childless widow of their deceased brother and have children by her in order to assure the posterity of the brother's name. In a hypothetical case seven brothers in turn married a woman, in turn were childless, and in turn were all survived by her. In the resurrection, the Sadducees asked in jest, to whom would she be married?

Since the Pentateuch stood supreme in its authoritative role, and since the Pentateuch contains no reference to the resurrection, the conclusion the Sadducees drew seemed inescapable. (See also Acts 4:1–2.) There was nothing beyond death. Through their innovative interpretation of Scripture, the Pharisees claimed to find evidence in the Pentateuch for belief in the resurrection. Deuteronomy 4:4 reads, "You who held fast to the LORD your God are all alive this day." The Pharisees interpreted this to refer to the fathers who had died and yet were still alive—they had been raised to life. Such liberal interpretations of the Pentateuch, however, were immediately ruled out by the strict readings of the Sadducees.

Unfortunately, we have no writings directly from the hands of the Sadducees. We may learn about them only from secondary accounts left by their critics. Moreover, with the destruction of the temple and the Roman occupation in 70 C.E., the Sadducees, who were so intimately associated with that powerful institution, disappear from view. We can better understand the conflicts reported in the New Testament with the Sadducees, however, if we fix on their role as protectors of the cult and the sanctity of the temple and its worship.

The occupation of positions associated with temple worship guaranteed them a powerful role in the Roman provincial government and in important Jewish institutions such as the Sanhedrin. Their position of power and prestige, of privilege and opportunity, as well as their role as guardians of the sanctity of the temple and conservators of religious interpretation brought them into sharp conflict with other Jewish groups, including the Christians. The early Christians remembered Jesus' rather casual attitude about the cult; they recalled his prophetic "cleansing" of the temple; they told stories critical of priests, some of whom were Sadducees, and of those in positions of wealth and power.

Doubtless such statements reflect some concerns of Jesus as well as the later period when the church was suffering reprisals for its harsh critique of a prevailing symbol system. It is fair to say, however, that the Sadducees sought to preserve the centrality of the temple, the law of the cult, and the sanctity of the land under trying circumstances. They worked to maintain the relative independence of Judea and the temple religion while at the same time maintaining good relations with Rome. This precarious balance was not easy to preserve. Their numbers were small, but their lofty and respected positions gave them enormous advantage in the institutions which framed the context of Jesus' life and of the early church.

The Scribes (an appended note)

The Scribes (Hebrew *sopher*), literally one who can cipher (*saphar*) or write, were the professional scholars of the first century. They knew the Torah; they could copy or write sections of Scriptures; they could offer authoritative interpretations of the sacred traditions; they even rendered judgments according to the Torah. Scribes occupied important seats in the halls of justice, especially the Sanhedrin, and like doctors of philosophy in our time, they rendered informed and authoritative interpretations of religious traditions. By virtue of their learning and function in the society they enjoyed the adulation and esteem of most Jewry. Both the Pharisees and Sadducees had scribes—i.e., specialists in law interpretation. Thus although strictly speaking the scribes were not a party within Judaism—but rather specialists within larger forms of religious expression—because of their prominence in the Gospel narrative a brief note on them here is apposite.

The scribal profession proudly traced its descent back to Ezra in the mid-fifth century B.C.E., who in the popular memory was the father of post-exilic Judaism. Ezra, we may recall, was the priest who returned from Babylonian captivity around 458 B.C.E., gathered the people before the "Water Gate" in Jerusalem, and read the "whole law" as a part of a covenant renewal ceremony. Ezra, so we are told, was a "scribe skilled in the law of Moses" (Ezra

7:6; see also 7:11). However, even before the Exile (597–537 B.C.E.) scribes were associated with the temple, teaching priests and Levites who in turn taught laymen. Later in the hellenistic period, from the third century B.C.E. on, when many scribes resisted the creeping influence of an alien culture, the need among laymen to take an active role to counter the allure of a great, cosmopolitan Greek culture pried the scribes loose from their traditionally intimate association with the temple priests. By the first century the Gospel of Mark refers explicitly to the "scribes of the Pharisees" (Mark 2:16; my translation) who were thus distinguished from scribes associated with the Sadducees.

Shortly before the Maccabean period (167–142 B.C.E.), the Wisdom of the scribe Jesus, the son of Sirach, was written and later translated into Greek by a grandson (around 132 B.C.E.). In this collection, Ecclesiasticus as it is known in Latin, we find a hymn which praises the scribe (38:24—39:11). A part of the hymn is sufficient to illustrate the importance of the scribe to pre-Christian Judaism:

> he [the scribe] who devotes himself
> to the study of the law of the Most High
> will seek out the wisdom of the ancients,
> and will be concerned with the prophecies;
> he will preserve the discourse of notable men
> and penetrate the subtleties of parables;
> he will seek out the hidden meanings of proverbs
> and be at home with the obscurities of parables.
> He will serve among great men and appear before rulers;
> he will travel through the lands of foreign nations,
> for he tests the good and the evil among men.
> He will set his heart to rise early
> to seek the Lord who made him,
> and will make supplication before the Most High. . . .
> If the great Lord is willing, he will be filled with the Spirit of understanding;
> he will pour forth words of wisdom and give thanks to the Lord in prayer. . . .
> He will reveal instruction in his teaching
> and will glory in the law of the Lord's covenant.
> Many will praise his understanding,
> and it will never be blotted out.(39:1–9)

The esteem accorded this learned scribe in the second century B.C.E. was doubtless enjoyed by the first-century scribe as well. In Mark's Gospel Jesus scorns the trappings associated with the scribal profession—the special garb that set them apart, the respectful greetings heaped on them in the market place, the seats of honor in the synagogues, and the special favor paid them at the feasts (Mark 12:38–39). Their association with Jerusalem in 3:22 lends their mission to question Jesus an official character. Mark repeatedly contrasts the "authority" of Jesus' teaching and his ministry with the conventional authority of the scribes—for example, 1:22. Such a juxtaposition makes sense only if the position of the scribes were a lofty, authoritative one.

References to the scribes in Mark's Gospel are uniformly negative, reflecting disputes between the church and the synagogue over scriptural interpretation. Mark echoes the traditional charge that the scribes played a key role in the accusations against Jesus that led to his death.

Matthew shares Mark's view with one exception. Ironically, in 13:52 many modern scholars see an autobiographical reference to the author himself: "every *scribe* who has been trained for the kingdom of heaven is like a householder who brings out of his treasure what is new and what is old" (my emphasis). The suspicion is that Matthew combines the new and old as a Christian scribe to frame his Gospel. And in Luke's Acts we also find one positive allusion to the scribes. In 23:9 we are told that the "scribes of the Pharisees" defend the old Pharisee, Paul, finding him innocent of the charges against him.

More about the scribes in the first half of the first century is difficult to discover. It is inappropriate to attempt a reconstruction of the scribal function before 70 C.E. from traditions drawn from later Mishnaic materials. We learn little from Josephus about the scribes. We find that he studied and that by fourteen, he rather immodestly tells us, he had mastered the Torah, but we learn nothing about his scribal teachers. It does seem likely that scribes belonged to the Sanhedrin, the highest court of the land, and that some scribes were Pharisees and other Sadducees, but to say Sanhedrin members were exclusively scribes is conjectural.[11] Whether "ordained" scribes were always called rabbi, a title of respect, is possible though not demonstrable.

In the Wisdom of Jesus ben Sirach we find that the scribe is expected to meditate on secrets of the tradition (39:7), but must we conclude that the scribes were guardians of an esoteric, Jewish mystical tradition? Again we are faced with uncertainty. We do know that they came from the ranks of both the Pharisees and Sadducees, of their intimate association with Torah, the treasure of Israel's sacred story, and of the key role they played in scriptural interpretation and rendering judicial decisions based on Torah. It is these functions that figure prominently in the New Testament dialogue. A sensitivity to their importance for first-century Jewish life may help us appreciate the points at issue in the New Testament narrative.

The Essenes

In the spring of 1947, Muhammad ed Dib, the young son of a Bedouin, struck out looking for a lost sheep on the Northwest corner of the Dead Sea. Before he found the sheep he discovered a cave in which a large number of Hebrew scrolls had been placed in large clay jars over 1800 years earlier. Now we know they were hidden there by a priestly community bracing for the Roman onslaught in the war of 66–70 c.e. After the initial discovery treasure hunters fanned out over the hills to find other stashes of scrolls. Many complete manuscripts were found and portions or fragments of hundreds of other scrolls, both canonical and noncanonical, were collected.

Archeologists later fully excavated the ruins nearby, establishing a solid link between the scrolls and the Qumran community (named after the Wadi Qumran). The layout of the ruins confirmed the picture sketched in the scrolls. The community, firmly ensconsed on a plateau overlooking the Dead Sea, was built to support their isolated, independent lifestyle. A complex water system providing reservoirs and ritual baths formed the heart of the physical surroundings. But there was also a kitchen, a pottery, a scriptorium for copying sacred texts, a refectory, laundry, pantry, assembly hall, and even a stable. The lack of sleeping quarters suggests the sectarians slept elsewhere, perhaps in caves nearby. A cemetery lay just to the east of the settlement.

No discovery has so revolutionized our understanding of first-century Judaism or early Christianity as this one. Although few would see any direct borrowing from the Qumran Scrolls in the New Testament, the worldview of the Qumran sect was typical of a type of Jewish piety that at least indirectly influenced many New Testament writings.

What we earlier had learned from Josephus and Philo about the Essenes is now largely confirmed firsthand by the Scrolls themselves (see Philo, *Every Good Man Is Free* 75–91 and Josephus, *War* 2:119–61 and *Antiquities* 18:18–22). Philo, a first-century writer in Alexandria tells us that the Essenes lived in communes away from the noxious moral climate of the town, that the communities aimed to be self-supporting through their own craftsmanship and agriculture (76) and gave up their claim to private property upon entering the community (78), living from a common purse (86). Following the injunction of Isaiah 40:3, "In the wilderness, prepare the way of the Lord," they had come to the wasteland to wait for the end. In the interim, according to Philo, they espoused pacifism, neither making nor using weapons of war (78). In the disciplined life of the community they learned the common rule, were instructed in the Scriptures, met for worship on the sabbath in their synagogue(!), shared common meals and cared for the sick and aged (80–91).

Josephus goes beyond Philo in opening a window on the daily lives of the Essenes and the "virtues" they practiced. Rising to pray before dawn, dispersing to their crafts and agricultural tasks until the fifth hour (eleven a.m.), they then reconvened, ritually bathed, and donned sacred white garments for the communal meal. The common meal was liturgically ordered by prayers both before and after (*War* 2:128–131). As the *Manual of Discipline* says, "When they have set the table to eat, or (prepared) the wine to drink, the priest shall first stretch out his hand to pronounce a blessing on the first-fruits of bread and wine" (1 QS 6:5–6).[12] Although the meal may not have been sacramental, it certainly possessed a high religious significance. In the "love feasts" of the New Testament we may see a meal that functions in much the same manner for the church. In the community rule we also learn that each able bodied member of the sect was to stand watch "in common for a third of all the nights of the year, to read the Book and study the law and bless in common" (6:7–8). During the three watches of the night when a portion of the community was always on station, the law was recited and interpreted and prayers were said.

Membership in the community came in three stages. Initiation was followed by one year of probation. Then after the successful completion of a rigorous examination the initiate was a novice for two years, followed by a second examination and admission as a full member. As a sign of completion of the trial period the member was given the white linen robe and allowed to share in the common meal. Now the "brother" must keep himself in a holy state of readiness for the imminent Day of the Lord.

A strict ethic was prescribed to secure this state of purity. The sect eschewed slavery, and with few exceptions marriage. They devoted themselves to the simple life and observed the sabbath commandment strictly. Their rigorous observance of sabbath law precluded lighting a fire, food preparation, or even defecation on this holy day. All bodily functions were made subservient to the holy discipline, sleeping and waking, working and praying, eating and eliminating.

Josephus found their zeal amazing. They followed the injunction in Deuteronomy 23:12–14, so he says, when "they dig a hole one foot deep. . . . They squat there, covered by their mantles so as not to offend the rays of God. Then they push back the excavated soil into the hole. . . . However natural the evacuation of excrement, they are accustomed to wash themselves afterwards as though defiled" (War 2:147–149). The prohibitions against oaths, spitting or sleeping in the holy assembly, ridiculing laughter, lying about one's possessions, and exposing one's nakedness may sound overly scrupulous to us, but for those sectarians these holy habits were a necessary part of readying themselves for God's final visitation.

This rigid, communal discipline was enforced by a priestly hierarchy. A priest in a position of supreme authority presided over all of the "camps." Each camp contained ten persons directed also by a priest (the Damascus Document, hereafter CD 14:6–12).[13] The community did contain laymembers, and some of them held positions of authority and influence. The bursar who managed the community's purse may have been a layman. Also a lay-Messiah, or Nasi, would, they expected, govern the community in the final days (The War Scroll, hereafter 1 QM; see 5:1). Unquestionably, though, the traditions, governance, and outlook were priestly in character. Priestly figures dictated the direction the community would take. Even the lay-Messiah was to be accompanied by a priestly Messiah.

The Writings from Qumran

After the initial sensational discovery of the scrolls and the later finds of whole and fragmentary manuscripts, the task of matching fragments, publication, and translation became an ongoing task continuing into the present. Except for Esther, at least a portion of every canonical book in the Hebrew Scriptures was found at Qumran. In addition scrolls dealing with community discipline and worship, scriptural interpretation, apocalypses, the location of buried treasure, horoscopes, and many other subjects were recovered. A brief survey of the nature and content of some of these scrolls may help the reader appreciate the significance of these materials for New Testament study.

1. *The Manual of Discipline (1 QS)* was found preserved almost in its entirety. It contained the liturgy and rubrics for worship, for a covenant renewal ceremony, and for a service of initiation into the community. It also included rules for corporate and individual conduct. A penal code prescribed a limited expulsion from the community for anyone who, for instance, "answers his fellow disrespectfully, or speaks (to him) impatiently" (one year, 1 QS 6:26–27), "for whoever interrupts the words of another," (10 days, 1 QS 7:10), and for "whoever laughs stupidly (and) loudly" (30 days, 6:14). The manual divides all human beings into two camps—good and evil. All people belong either to the "children of light" or the "children of darkness." An unbridgeable chasm separates those loyal to the spirit of Truth from the disciples of the spirit of Falsehood (3:13—4:26).

2. *The Damascus Document (CD)* was first found in the Ezra Synagogue in Cairo in 1896. It was called the *Damascus* Document because the scroll locates the community in the land of Damascus. Portions of the document suggest that it almost certainly originated at Qumran. Essentially, it contains the story of the origin of the community, the conflict between the Teacher of Righteousness, the community's founder, and the Wicked Priest, doubtless a high priest in Jerusalem against whom the Teacher rebelled.

3. *The Hymn Scroll (1 QH)*, which contains moving Hebrew poetry similar to that of the Psalms, attempts to capture the whole range of human experience. This collection offered the members of the community an appropriate language of joy and sorrow, pain and delight, and of lamentation and joyous song.

4. *The War Scroll (1 QM)* gives an elaborate, detailed description of the final eschatological battle between the "sons of light" and the "sons of darkness," between God's holy angel, Michael, and the agent of evil, Belial. The description of the military strategy to be employed is sketched in graphic detail. The battle formation, weapons, and even the standards for the final, decisive holy war are described exactly. The sect clearly expected on that day

to emerge victorious over all of the enemies of God including the Kittim (or Romans) and the wicked, unrepentant priests in Jerusalem.

5. *The Pesherim* (e.g., 1 *QpHab*)[14] or commentaries on biblical texts abound at Qumran. Not only did the community meticulously copy and preserve the holy writings, they also wrote commentaries on the sacred texts. We think of modern commentaries as studies of a passage in *its* context. But, the Qumran community had little interest in the objective, historical study of Scripture. They read texts as if they anticipated the future of the community. Since the Scriptures were believed to embrace the future of the sect, a dynamic relationship was established between Israel's ancient, sacred story and the time of the sect. The past provided a window into the future, and the future provided a lens for viewing the writings of the past. The texts therefore were always resplendent with mystery and possibility. It was in this spirit that commentaries were written on Habakkuk, Nahum, Genesis, Psalm 37, et al.

6. *The Temple Scroll* only recently has been published in English translation. Because of the initial conflict between the Teacher of Righteousness and the temple priesthood—the belief of the community that the corrupt temple cult must be replaced by a purified one—the community had to redefine its relationship to the temple. *The Temple Scroll* fulfills this function, offering instructions for ritualistic cleanness, sacred festivals, the shape and function of the temple in the New Age, and a description of the eschatological king of Israel and his army.

In addition to these works fragments of other types of materials were also found. Portions of *Targums*—that is, loose renditions of biblical texts in Aramaic—came to light, as well as fragments of Greek texts. This broad array of texts when supplemented with the writings of Josephus and Philo provides sufficient information to make a quite detailed composite drawing of the Hebrew religion at Qumran.

Theological Perspectives

1. *Dualism.* The Qumran sectarians believed they were witnesses of a climactic, cosmic struggle between Michael's angels and Belial's hosts, between God and the Evil One—between the forces of light and the powers of darkness. This universal, brutal conflict will penetrate the heart of the society as well as the soul of each individual. The angel of light will be pitted against the angel of darkness. The Teacher of Righteousness will stand opposite the Wicked Priest in Jerusalem. The "pure thing of the Many,"—i.e., the community—will oppose the outside agents of corruption and impurity. The "children of light" will be locked in mortal struggle with the "children of darkness." This radical dichotomy allows no middle ground and no compro-

mise, accommodation, or negotiation with the forces of evil. Like the Christian Apocalypse which exhorts all to be either hot or cold, for the lukewarm will be spewed out, so these Scrolls allow no room for moderation. As the community rule so aptly says, "Dominion over all the sons of righteousness is in the hand of the Prince of light; they walk in the ways of light. All dominion over the sons of perversity is in the hand of the Angel of darkness; they walk in the ways of darkness" (*1 QS* 3:20–21). There is no mediating class of people between these two extremes.

According to the scrolls the "sons of light"[15] will receive "perpetual life" (*1 QS* 4:7–8) while the "sons of darkness" will endure "the disgrace of destruction by the fire of the regions of darkness" (*1 QS* 4:12–13). Although the in-group out-group opposition reflects the cosmic struggle, the insiders are not exempt from first hand acquaintance with evil. For, as they put it, God "allotted unto man two Spirits that he should walk in them until the time of His Visitation; they are the Spirits of truth and perversity" (*1 QS* 3:18–19). The difference between the two camps, however, is that though the sons of light sometimes stumble, they finally rely on the "God of Israel and His Angel of truth" for succour and renewal. While the "sons of darkness," true to their nature, are agents of evil perpetually out of blind necessity.

It is easy to detect New Testament parallels to the Qumran dualism. In Paul's letters in particular we see how this fierce cosmic conflict is experienced in the heart of each believer as it was at Qumran. The struggle between God and "the ruler of this world" is matched by the ferocious tussle between the Spirit and flesh in bondage to evil. Moreover, in Paul's letters as at Qumran there are two classes of people—"sons of light" and children "of darkness" (1 Thess. 5:5; see also John 12:36). In Paul's Epistles as in the Dead Sea Scrolls the battle between the cosmic powers was viewed as a premonitory sign of the approaching end. Both Jesus and Paul, like the Qumran sect, believed they were living in the final days of the world. The tension and sense of urgency created by this imminent expectation had momentous implications for conduct and the interpretation of sacred tradition.

Integrated with the eschatological outlook of the community was the expectation of two Messiahs, a priestly Messiah of Aaron, and a royal Messiah of David (*1 QS* 9:11; *Florilegium* 1:11–13). The sectarians expected this Davidic Messiah would humiliate all enemies of the community, both Jewish and Gentile. Drawing on Isaiah 11:1–5, the sectarians proclaim that the new David will "rule over all the nations and Magog [. . . and al]l the people his sword will judge (them)." His authority and style of rule shall be learned from the priests: "[. . . a]s they teach him, so will he judge" (see the *Commentary on Isaiah, 1 QpIsa* frag. D, vss. 4–7.) That is, he will rule, counsel, and establish the righteous who are oppressed. The coming of a prophet was also expected to accompany the advent of the two Messiahs although his role, though important, was overshadowed by that of the Messiahs. These three figures, then, each reflective of some Jewish tradition of expectation and hope, merge into one figure in the New Testament description of Jesus.

Paul and the author of the Gospel of Mark, like the sectarians, expected imminent judgment. This "visitation" implied vindication for the righteous and damnation for the wicked. In Matthew 19:28 and in 1 Corinthians 6:2 are reflected a belief similar to that of the Qumran community. It was believed that the faithful would share in the judging function (see *1 QpHab* 5:4, "God will judge all nations by the hand of His elect"). Punishments reserved for the Jews who harassed God's elect are especially severe. The words of *1 QS* 2:15 threaten the wicked Jerusalem priests and Levites with eternal fire.

The accomplices of the Wicked Priest who committed outrages against the "elect of God" will taste a fiery judgment (*1 QpHab* 10:13). Perverse Jews who insulted the community were promised destruction and denied posterity (*1 QS* 5:12). Qumran shares with the New Testament the concept of judgment and the volatile language of the end—wrath, fire, a dismantling of the world, etc., though such a common outlook and language hardly need suggest a direct tie. That feverish expectation of the end was shared by many fringe movements in first-century Jewish life.

2. *The Righteousness of God.* In the Qumran texts, as in Paul's Epistles, we see an emphasis on the righteousness of God. In first-century Jewish piety, *sedaqah*, the Hebrew word for righteousness, refers not to an inward ethical quality but to a relationship established by God between himself and his people. Moreover, righteousness in both Qumran and the letters of Paul was eschatological in nature. Associated with God's wondrous deeds at the end of history, God's righteous work toward his own was an act of mercy to be gratefully appropriated by faith. Although the inhabitants of Qumran cultivated a devotion to the law, they nevertheless understood their salvation to depend on God's grace, not on observance of this law. As the *Manual of Discipline* says:

> For to God belongs my justification,
> and the perfection of my way,
> and the uprightness of my heart are in his hand:
> by His righteousness are my rebellions blotted out.

(*1 QS* 11:2–3)

Keenly aware of their own sin the sectarians, like Paul, appealed to God's mercy for their salvation:

We have been sinful, we have rebelled,
We have sinned, we have been wicked. . . .
But He extends his gracious mercy toward us
    for ever and ever. (*1 QS* 1:24–25; 2:1; see also the *Hymn Scroll* [1 QH] 4:35–
    40; 13:16–21; 9:28–35)

In this reliance on God's mercy for their salvation, the covenanters stand squarely in the Old Testament tradition. But, in light of many modern caricatures of Judaism as a legalistic religion, it is valuable to have this corrective material contemporaneous with the birth of the New Testament.

3. *Terms and Practices.* In addition to the similarity of theological outlook, the early church and the sectarians share some terminology and practices. The reference to "the poor" in both the New Testament and Qumran makes an association between the humble, pious folk waiting empty handed for God's kingdom and God's chosen (Matt. 5:2; *1 QM* 13:14; CD 1:9). In both, the insiders possess a secret wisdom unknown to the outsiders (Mark 4:11; *1 QH* 13:14; 12:13). The term "covenant" designated a faithful relationship between God and his people for both. Discipline by exclusion from the community was practiced by both the Dead Sea community and the early church. In both holy meals were communal, and it is possible that a voluntary, communal use of goods was practiced by both groups (Acts 2:44–45; 4:34–35; 5:1–11; as well as the *Manual of Discipline*). Paul's own preference for celibacy may share an understanding also known at Qumran. Both expected the arrival of the end to be preceded by a period of great trauma. In the face of the impending distress both may have foregone the normal, wholesome domestic joys to devote themselves, like the soldier in holy war, to the fierce struggle at hand.

The terminology and practices noted here were perhaps known to many pious, Jewish groups of the first century. The Qumran usage, however, documents how such a constellation of terms, cultic action and communal behavior received expression in a specific Jewish community of the first century. This collection is valuable because it illumines the background of many of the views expressed and many of the actions encouraged by the early Christians.

While there are similarities in the End-expectation of the church and the Essenes, the two do diverge at other points. The covenanters of Qumran withdrew into the "wilderness" to prepare for the end; no such separation is evident in the early church. A cultic purity was enforced in the community in preparation for Yahweh's final visitation. The church, however, displayed a relaxed attitude toward the laws of purity. The priestly cult at Qumran quite naturally expected that in the end a purified cult would replace the corrupted order in a real, earthly temple; the church and its Galilean constituents harbored no such expectation. (Although a spiritualized cult does appear in

Paul's Romans 12:1, in Hebrews, and in parts of the book of Revelation, the imagery derived from the temple does not anticipate an association with an eschatological temple in the Jerusalem of the future.)

The Qumran sectarians expected to be actively involved as soldiers in God's final battle for the world; the church on the other hand claimed no such physical participation in the coming apocalyptic warfare. At Qumran daily water lustrations cleansed the community for its purified life together; baptism for the church symbolized a cleansing also but its tie with the initiation into the community made it a singular event. A general resurrection finds no explicit reference in the Qumran texts but is a general feature of the New Testament expectation. The community is admonished to love the sons of light and hate the sons of darkness (1 QS 1:9f.), whereas both the gospel tradition and Paul urge love of the insider *and* the outsider (enemy). (John 15:12, however, resembles the Qumran emphasis to love the insider.) True to its temple interests, the retarded, handicapped, crippled, diseased, blind, deaf, and women were excluded from the holy assembly. The New Testament tells us that Jesus welcomed those who would have been excluded from Qumran.

Although direct ties are difficult to establish between the Qumran sect and the New Testament, the scrolls are of great value in giving a description of a type of Jewish expression and piety in the first century that shared many features of belief and practice with the early church. An understanding of these background elements can help us better understand both the church's dependence on its mother faith and its departures from it.

Zealots and Sicarii

To repeat the account of the political struggles of the Zealots and Sicarii presented in chapter one is unnecessary. Yet since the engine that drove that revolt was powered by religious symbols and traditions, a brief summary of those elements is desirable.

The roots of the animating zeal for the Zealot movement are found in the Old Testament. The radical interpretation of the Shema—"Hear, O Israel, the Lord our God, the Lord is one" (Deut. 6:4)—had historically been a part of Israel's self-experience. Zeal for Yahweh's holiness and honor led Moses to slay unrepentant worshipers of the golden calf (Exod. 32:25–29). The grandson of Aaron (Phinehas) zealously guarded the purity of the community and averted the wrath of Yahweh by killing a Jewish man and the Midianite woman he had taken as his consort (Num. 25:6–9). The Old Testament settlement traditions abound in references to holy war in which zeal for Yahweh dictated total destruction of the enemy and his property (e.g., Num. 31:13–20, where only young girls were spared).

The awareness that they were an elect people receiving the promised land as an act of grace was also a vital ingredient in the faith of those zealous for Yahweh. Since God gave Israel exclusive claim to the land, zealous Jews believed any occupation by the Romans or any other alien power violated Yahweh's design. The system of taxation imposed by the Emperor, no matter how progressive, was bound to stoke the smoldering fires of resentment. Since the land belonged to Israel and Israel alone, any tax, whatever its size, transgressed deeply held religious convictions. Such zeal naturally inspired a venomous hatred against those who accommodated themselves to the foreign domination. Many held tax collectors, for example, in special contempt. The Pharisees in Mark roundly spurned Jesus for eating and consorting with tax collectors whom they lumped with sinners (2:15–17). Further, the fact that Matthew himself was recruited by Jesus from among this profession was reason enough for such Jews to look down on Jesus and his followers. Some disfavor would naturally attach to a group of disciples containing a tax collector.

The priests and Sadducees also were actively scorned by many. Their positions of leadership made compromise with the Romans necessary for an orderly state of civil affairs. Yet many zealous country folk, already burdened by the Roman taxes and resentful, counted as betrayal any act of accommodation. And the material profit the priests and Sadducees gained from their cooperation with the Romans only served to further inflame popular opinion against them.

Wherever the holiness of the law or the sanctity of the temple were threatened with defilement, the zealous were under an obligation to resist. And, since the temple was in the hands of an establishment obliged to the Romans, conflict was inevitable. The Romans controlled custody and use of the high priest's vestments, which enabled them to symbolically manage the sacred cult. The right to name or influence the appointment of a high priest friendly towards Rome gave the Emperor even greater power over this hagiarchy which unquestionably constituted a central feature of Israel's life.

The daily sacrifices offered by the priests on behalf of the Emperors gave religious support and legitimacy to the Roman occupation. In addition the permanent assignment of Roman troops to the citadel adjacent to the temple complex to "control the crowds" also rankled pious Jews. And the periodic insults and abuse heaped on pilgrims in Jerusalem for the festivals by insensitive or boorish Roman troops only further fanned the flames of revolt. Many zealous Jews felt the temple had been compromised, and it was their duty to defend and restore its sanctity, even if it cost them their lives.

Conditions were ripe for a prophetic or messianic figure who would mobilize this righteous indignation to "liberate" Jerusalem from the Romans, purge the temple of the pollution caused by a compromised ("unclean") priesthood, revoke the unholy taxes, and restore religious and political independence to Israel. The memory of the heroic Maccabees, coupled with the holy war tradition and a rising apocalyptic fever, emboldened the zealous to join in an act of violent defense of their institutions and land. The dry tinder was sparked into a conflagration in 66 C.E. The temple was taken and "purged" and Jerusalem was reclaimed. But the revolt came to a chilling end in the year 70 when the Roman Legions broke through Jerusalem's defenses and put a torch to the city.

Martin Hengel has convincingly shown that Jesus was no revolutionary.[16] But neither Jesus, his followers, nor the early church could be unaffected by the conditions behind the revolt—the festering resentments, the violent episodic protests, the humiliation and shame experienced by their countrymen, or the contempt held for the priests and Sadducees. The alert reader will see in the Gospels traces of Jewish rancor toward the Romans, and the *animus* of some Jews toward others who weakly accepted Roman domination. Though a minority movement, the impulses behind the rise of the Zealots, the conditions fostering such religious zeal, and the fanatical defense of Israel's sacred symbols touched all people in Israel as well as Jews in the Diaspora.

ʿAm ha-ʾaretz

In spite of the powerful influence exerted on Israel's public and private piety by the forms of religious expression just noted, most Israelites professed no membership in any one of the "parties" above. The great majority of these folk were ʿam ha-ʾaretz, a Hebrew term for people of the land. They certainly did not deny Judaism or repudiate either the written or oral law, but they were called people of the land because they were not as scrupulous as others in observing some commandments (especially the laws of purity), and they were ignorant of much of the content of the Torah and shunned its study. The ʿam ha-ʾaretz tended to be farmers or a part of the peasant population, though theoretically any person from any socio-economic level could be of the ʿam ha-ʾaretz. They were the ordinary people, the masses, from both the city and the country. They were doubtless shunned and ridiculed by those who were scrupulous about the laws of purity, observing the tithe and the study of Torah, namely the Pharisees, Sadducees, and Essenes. Later rabbinic tradition advised against permitting one's daughter to marry an ʿam ha-ʾaretz since he was considered nothing but a sexual animal—or worse yet, exactly like a Gentile![17] Rabbi Judah ha-Nasi, it is reported, once opened his storehouse of food to his countrymen in a time of famine, but barred the ʿam ha-ʾaretz from entering.[18] It is likely that even in Jesus' day not only were the ʿam ha-ʾaretz considered inferior but ritually unclean, and therefore contaminating to a person in a state of religious purity.

The testimony of the Gospels is nearly unanimous in affirming that Jesus freely associated with and indeed found most of his followers among the "people of the land." He pitied them because they were like sheep without a shepherd (Mark 6:34). Some of Jesus' disciples ate with unwashed hands—that is, ritually impure—in the manner of the *'am ha-'aretz*. Jesus clearly took the side of the *'am ha-'aretz* against the scribes and Pharisees (see Mark 7:1–23), and his association with the lepers, handicapped, and sinners suggests his concern for those outside the pale of traditional religious expression, or for those suffering exclusion and prejudice.[19]

Hellenistic Piety

Though Jesus was a Jew, preached a Jewish gospel to other Jews, and though the earliest church was largely composed of Jewish Christians, the influence of the Greek world on New Testament writings was thoroughly pervasive. The language of the New Testament was Greek, the form of the Epistles follows the structure of the hellenistic letter, and many of the traditions found therein come from hellenistic circles. Vocabulary, concepts, metaphors, and cultic acts from the Greeks inform much of the New Testament. The mingling of these two cultures in this respect is widely recognized. Less widely acknowledged, however, is the influence of hellenistic piety on the world in which the New Testament evolved. Some authors of New Testament books as well as those they addressed were directly exposed to the influence of hellenistic religious values. Paul's addressees, Luke's readers, the churches of the Deutero-Pauline writings, all these would have known hellenistic piety first hand (see especially 1 Cor. 8:1–13; 10:14–22; 1 Thess. 1:9). Our consideration of the New Testament context therefore requires at least a brief survey of some of those religious options.

Before Alexander's body was cold in the grave the empire he built was beginning to crumble. Even after a generation of civil war defined the major divisions of the empire, factional rivalries continued. Eventually the kingdoms carved out by Alexander's generals collapsed into hostile camps. The synthesis imposed on the Middle East from Egypt to India dissolved. City fought city. Democratic institutions languished. Military rule undermined the city-state. Courts became corrupt and impotent. A stubborn economic depression aggravated the agony brought on by hunger and starvation. Infanticide, widely practiced, accelerated the population decline. This vortex of upheaval exacerbated the growing skepticism about traditional religion and the ability of the gods to save humankind from its desperate plight. Vestiges of folk religion remained and forms of individualistic piety devoted to some minor deity survived, but traditional beliefs waned or became diluted. In the place of the Olympian gods, people sought the reassurance of impersonal, divine forces ordering the cosmos.

With this growing cynicism came a darkness of spirit that eclipsed the glorious achievements of earlier Greek philosophy and culture. The reverence for beauty and order and the celebration of the body in art and sculpture were dramatically altered by a depreciation of the world followed by a renunciation of the body as form. Coupled with this declining interest in the world came also a devaluation of hard rational thought and interest in science.[20] The concept of *oecumene*, the dream of *one* world in which all people lived as kin, soured. Consequently the Greeks were thrown back on their resources of piety, visions, and private wisdom. To some of those forms of piety we now turn.

The Mystery Religions

The mystery religions promised liberation from a bleak landscape. Certain esoteric rites joined the initiate in an ecstatic union with the god, offering visions of another world and providing escape from a chaotic landscape. With the steady decline of public institutions and traditional religion, interest in the mysteries grew. Some mysteries, such as the Isis cult or the Dionysian rites, were imported versions of nature religions.

Isis was an Egyptian goddess and consort of Osiris, a dying and rising god linked to the rise and fall of the Nile, the fermentation of wine, the leavening of bread, and the abundance of harvests. Dionysus, a dying and rising god native to Asia Minor, likewise assured the fermentation of wines and the fertility of the earth.[21] Those intoxicated with his ambrosial drink were transported into the divine realm and through his orgiastic rites many felt directly touched by the power and mystery of the god. Together these deities assured the fertility of the earth and the order of the world.

Rooted in an agricultural context, these mysteries celebrated the death and resurrection of the god in synchrony with seedtime and harvest. Through these and other secret rites the celebrant merged with the cosmic order. Transplanted to an urban setting, however, these mysteries functioned no longer to activate a dormant earth but to deliver those craving release from public disaster, private futility, and individual estrangement. In the ritualistic enactment of the death of the god the initiate died, and in the resurrection of the god the initiate rose up from a decaying world to share the mystery of life. Since for many the rites transposed despair into ecstasy, suffering to joy, and imprisonment to release, their success is understandable.

Stoicism

In the tumultuous cauldron of the third century B.C.E., Stoicism took shape. That period of historical terror flung insistent questions to the foreground of the religious thought of the times: if the gods exist and if they care, why, some asked, do they ignore human suffering so multiplied by war and famine? If they are just, why do the gods allow the poor to be robbed by the powerful, and good people to be brutalized by the evil ones? Although the traditional gods had no place in Stoic philosophy, a divine presence, if not a divine personality, was still affirmed. Instead of Zeus, for example, stood the divine principle *Logos* controlling the cosmos, permeating all that existed.

Since *Logos* was thought to control all destiny, all events, all fortune and misfortune, always serving some divine purpose, evil was necessarily viewed as good merely disguised. This view is best articulated by Cleanthes, an early Stoic from the third century B.C.E.:

> For nought is done on earth apart from thee,
> Nor in thy vault of heaven, nor in the sea. . . .
> But skill to make the crooked straight is thine,
> To turn disorder to a fair design
> Ungracious things are gracious in thy sight
> For ill and good thy power doth so combine.[22]

Chrysippus, another Stoic from the same period, saw this *Logos* as sovereign over all. Affirmation that all things serve a divine purpose was a central tenet of Stoic belief. Droughts, plagues, earthquakes, storms, debilitating illness, crippling accidents, or tragic death all serve some purpose. According to Chrysippus, even bed bugs (and presumably flies and mosquitoes also) support the divine *Logos* by keeping the sluggard from sleeping too late and too long. And mice teach us to be careful where we put things.

The test of Stoic confidence in the fundamental rationality of the universe came in the ability to accept everything with equanimity (or *apatheia*). Unlike the weak resignation suggested in its English cognate, *apatheia* indicated a sense of self-sufficiency and autonomy for the preoccupations and anxious cares afflicting others. The conviction that *Logos* turned misfortune to a good end insulated the Stoic from the cruel adversity and historical terror of the third century. Admittedly this disassociation from upheaval, coupled with an interest in the harmony between the *Logos* in each individual and in cosmic reason, eliminated any possibility of an interest in history. The Stoics' association with the timeless *Logos* detached them from all time and made any involvement with history superfluous.

In the New Testament, and especially in the Pauline letters, the Stoic influence on both the Apostle and his readers is evident. The diatribe, a method of argumentation using questions posed by a hypothetical objector, appears in such questions as "Are we to continue in sin that grace may abound?" (Romans 6:1); "What shall we say then? That the law is sin?" (Romans 7:7); and "Is there injustice on God's part?" (Romans 9:14).

The New Testament, however, unlike Stoicism is firmly anchored to history; it believes on a historical personage, draws from a rich past, and anticipates a historical future. Unlike the Stoics, who translate the concept of freedom into personal autonomy, Paul views freedom exclusively as salvation from the hostile powers of Sin and Death for obedience to Christ. Where the Stoic gains freedom through trust in *Logos* and *apatheia* Paul finds freedom as an eschatological gift from God. Though some of his terminology and rhetorical style may come from the Stoics, Paul differs in important ways. His readers, however, especially in Corinth, may share the Stoic contempt for the body and detachment from history.

Neo-Pythagoreanism

Because of its ability to synthesize diverse philosophical and religious traditions, Pythagoreanism enjoyed broad popular appeal in the first century. Tracing its origin back to the distinguished philosopher Pythagoras of the sixth century B.C.E., the Neo-Pythagoreans cultivated a sensitivity to the divine element within the self. Convinced of the truth of the ancient Pythagorean maxim, "Like seeks like," the Neo-Pythagoreans believed the godly element in each person was constantly straining to return to its divine source. By renouncing the flesh they sought to move the spark within toward the great, cosmic fire above. Vows of chastity, poverty, obedience, and silence effected liberation from the body and affirmed the divine within and above the self. Recognizing that a portion of the divine soul known to humanity is also lodged in other living creatures, the Neo-Pythagoreans were protective of all life. Out of respect for the divine ether in other animate life, they wore no leather or wool clothing, and they abstained from meat.

Seeking attunement or harmony with the divine, Neo-Pythagoreans were deeply mystical. Suffused with the divine they called themselves *Entheoi* (those in whom god dwells) and *Ekstatikoi* (those standing outside themselves in the spirit). This enthusiasm, literally infusion with God, broke through in miraculous deeds. In their view, mighty works gave proof of the divine power and presence, and authenticated the divine nature of the one performing them.[23]

This attunement to the divine element within sensitized the Neo-Pythagoreans to the divine element in the universe as well. They saw divine order in the regular motion of the planets and other heavenly bodies. This perception, not scientific curiosity, inspired their diligent study of astronomy. Believing the astral bodies were divine beings controlling all human destiny, the Neo-Pythagoreans observed their movements to learn their truth "as something at once beatific and comforting."[24] And thus was each person conceived as a being cradled in a universal harmony.

The magical quality that Neo-Pythagoreans assigned to numbers may strike some as strange, but their interest in mathematics was related to the sense of proportionality they discovered in the musical scale, in geometry, and in the study of astronomy. Since the movements of the planets were reducible to numbers, the quantitative ciphers took on some of the sacred character of the harmony they described. The balance between finity and infinity, between singular and plural, between odd and even numbers partook of the divine reality which directed the course of the stars and the paths of life on earth.

With its emphasis on harmony, its resolution of opposites, and its kinship of the sacred spark in the self with the divine element in the heavens, Neo-Pythagoreanism offered an alternative to the nihilistic philosophy which had developed among the Greeks regarding cruel Fate (*moira*), blind Chance (*tyche*), or dumb Necessity (*ananke*). To those trapped by mindless or careless forces amidst a swirl of war and upheaval, Neo-Pythagoreanism promised a way out. It offered a method of resolving human tragedy in a divine harmony, a way of overcoming alienation and loneliness with an emphasis on kinship with the divine, and a message of release from the tyranny of irrational and capricious forces. Given the broad popular appeal of this movement, the chances are it touched some of the communities the New Testament addresses, perhaps rather significantly.

Cynics

The Cynics proudly wore the epithet, "dog," (Greek *kuon*) contemptuously hung on them by their critics. Claiming freedom from the false values and cheap aspirations of the uncritical majority, the Cynics sought complete autonomy by stripping themselves of all concern for wealth, fashionable dress, sumptuous quarters, popularity, or family. Disdaining traditional learning, scornful of the deference shown the powerful and of the uncritical adulation of the great philosophers by their contemporaries, the Cynics aspired instead to the simple life.

Watching a child drink from cupped hands, Diogenes threw away his cup saying, "A child has beaten me in the plainness of living."[25] Sustained by begging, wandering like an exile, sleeping on his cloak, the Cynic counted himself most blest. "All things," Diogenes said, "belong to the gods. The gods are friends to the wise, and friends share all property in common; therefore, all things are the property of the wise. . . ."[26] Alexander the Great is reported to have said to Diogenes, "'Ask me any boon you like.' To which he replied, 'Stand out of my light.'"[27]

Understandably many found the Cynic behavior and philosophy revolting. Seneca, writing in the middle of the first century, scoffs at their "repellent attire, unkempt hair, slovenly beard, open scorn of silver dishes, a couch on the bare earth and . . . other perverted forms of self-display."[28] Whether these wandering critics directly influenced New Testament writings is disputed, but at the least some indirect pressure is likely. A word of caution is necessary, however.

Conceptual parallels offer no proof of borrowing. Concerns similar to those of the Cynics do appear in the New Testament. Luke's report that Jesus had "nowhere to lay his head," (9:58), or Jesus' command to the disciples in Mark to "take nothing for their journey . . . no bread, no bag, no money" (6:8), or the scorn heaped on those seeking public applause or security in "treasures" (Matt. 6:1–21), each superficially resembles Cynic concerns. But demonstrated links with distinctive language, peculiar phraseology, or unique actions, as well as geographical or cultural proximity, are required to make a case for borrowing. At points in the Pauline letters Cynic influence is demonstrable. Betz has shown Paul's list of his hardships (2 Cor. 11:23–29) closely parallels a similar catalogue in the Cynic diatribe.[29] Paul's understanding of the radical character of his style of mission may also contain some Cynic patterns. In any case, the sight of wandering Cynic philosophers understandably colored the way common folk viewed all itinerant missionaries, including peripatetic Christian preachers.

Gnosticism

Though not an independent movement in the first century, a gnostic idiom and mythology was already forming in Jewish and Christian circles. The later development of the movement confirmed tendencies already evident within the New Testament itself. Whether Gnosticism[30] came from Jewish or hellenistic circles is unclear. The movement did, however, reflect the profound alienation of much hellenistic piety and simultaneously produced a grotesque caricature of the Hebrew religion.

Most gnostic systems formed around a violent antagonism to this world. They held matter to be the evil work of an evil god. The Creator God of Genesis appears as a sinister being opposed to the true, high God. At the heart of gnosticism lay a radical dualism between the world above and the world below, between matter and spirit, between truth and falsehood, knowledge and ignorance, and light and darkness. This deprecation of the material world mightily influenced gnostic anthropology. Created by Yahweh—the evil god of this world—and drugged into a stupor blinding them to the divine spark within, the lost wandered aimlessly in perpetual ignorance. Except for the intervention of the high God who sent a Redeemer to awaken the lost from sleep, all creatures would have remained hopelessly lost. Once awakened, however, they recognized their heavenly citizenship; they *knew* their origin and destiny. The power of ignorance and the power of slavery were overcome by the power of the Redeemer. Liberated from their bondage by *gnosis*, the gnostics gave proof of this freedom by repudiating the physical body through ascetic vows, and showed their contempt for matter and their superiority over it by indulging the appetites. Sinning was one way of declaring one's salvation, for by breaking the rules made by the lower god, the gnostic demonstrated a superiority over the god of this world.

Certain gnostic tendencies appear in the New Testament, albeit in a less extreme form (see 1 Cor., the fourth Gospel, Col., and the pastoral Epistles, i.e., 1 and 2 Tim. and Titus). In 1 Corinthians we learn Paul's addressees claim to be wise, to possess knowledge, to be free, and to be already redeemed.[31] They strive to live above sexual distinctions, and in their "saved" state to stand above the Apostles and Scripture.

Their sense of deliverance from this world, their claim to knowledge and freedom, and their boast of complete salvation in the present conform with the dominant motifs of later gnostic myths. The dualism in the fourth Gospel between the world above and the world below, between light and darkness, and between truth and falsehood resembles the antagonistic division in Gnosticism. The author of Colossians combats a world-denying "heresy" bent on cosmic speculation some feel is gnostic.[32] The author of the Pastorals defends against a false teaching devoted to asceticism and eon speculation, to claiming a higher knowledge (*gnosis*), to encouraging libertine behavior, and to teaching a resurrection already experienced. The contours of this religious outlook also strongly resemble those of gnostic mythology.

Hellenistic Jewish Piety

Few Jews in the first century escaped the pull of hellenistic culture. Yet, Diaspora Jews (i.e., those dispersed, living outside of Palestine) were more open to the ways and outlook of Hellenism than were Palestinian Jews in general. The active interchange between cultures set in motion by Alexander's conquests made religious tolerance a political necessity—especially in the Greek cities scattered across the Middle East. Exclusive views gave way to ecumenism, and confrontation, to compromise. As stated so well by V. Tcherikover,

> It was quite impossible, living among the Greeks and enjoying the splendid works of Greek literature, to be enclosed in a spiritual Ghetto and to be reckoned among the "barbarians." It was a necessity to find a compromise, a synthesis, which would permit a Jew to remain a Jew and, at the same time, to belong to the elect society of the Greeks, the bearers of world culture.[33]

The influence of Hellenism touched Diaspora Judaism at many points. Even in the translation of the Hebrew Scriptures into Greek, an emphasis on tolerance crept into the text. In Exodus 22:28 where the Hebrew Scriptures read "You shall not revile *Elohim*" (the personal name of God, plural), the Greek has "You shall not revile *the gods*," thus encouraging tolerance of and respect for all forms of religious piety even when one did not subscribe to them. Similarly, the Letter of Aristeas, written by an Alexandrian Jew in the second century B.C.E., claims Yahweh, the God of Israel, is the same high God other peoples worship under different names. God, he says, "the Creator of all things, whom they (i.e., the Jews) worship is he, whom all men worship."[34]

After the Babylonian Exile (597–537 B.C.E.), the essential feature of Israel's covenant with Yahweh was law observance. Strict observance of circumcision and purity laws defined Israel's distinctiveness as a people apart. In the Diaspora, however, as Jews sought accommodation with their Gentile neighbors, the emphasis shifted from strict observance of laws underscoring Israel's particularity to participation in the glorious history of the Jews. As J. J. Collins has shown, to be Jewish in the Diaspora is:

> to belong to the same people as Abraham and Moses and the other heroes of the past. The exploits of these heroes show the preeminence of the Jews by outshining the heroes of the other peoples. At the same time the criteria for excellence are those commonly accepted in the Hellenistic world. The distinctly Jewish virtues of the Torah are thrust into the background.[35]

Thus the gulf between Hebrew religion and Hellenism narrowed. Even where an ethnic pride remained the line between Gentile and Jew was blurred. More and more, hellenistic Judaism welcomed and even actively sought Gentiles as converts. Baron may be correct in saying that Jewish missionaries traveled from city to city contending for the loyalty of their hearers.[36] There is evidence of their success. Gentiles attended synagogues, observed the Jewish sabbath, studied Torah, and gave children Jewish names. Consequently, the exchange between Jew and Gentile was reciprocal, and this interaction encouraged tolerance, respect, and in some cases mutual admiration.

Elsewhere we also see an openness to hellenistic views in the way the concept of the ideal Jew conformed to the hellenistic vision. Aristeas took prudence, justice, and temperance, Stoic marks of the ideal man, as characteristic of the ideal Jew as well. The rational process valued by the philosophers was also highly prized by educated Diaspora Jews, and the results were not always salutary. The elevation of reason at the expense of the physical world drove a wedge between higher reason and lower flesh. This emerging split between mind and matter, and the corresponding rupture between heaven and earth, stood behind the growing tendency to view matter in harshly negative terms. In the writings of Philo, a first-century Alexandrian Jew, one can see tension building between the positive assessment of the material world in the Hebrew Scriptures and its devaluation in Hellenism. Some of the same tensions may be seen in Paul's letters.

Although there was an accommodation to Hellenism among Diaspora Jews, it would be incorrect to speak of a general assimilation. To be sure, Jews spoke the Greek language, attended the theater, took education in the Greek classics, and were loyal subjects in the hellenistic political system; yet they did so without fatally compromising their ancestral religion. While national or ethnic pride led many Jews to hold their heads high among the Greek custodians of a great, cosmopolitan culture, at the same time they sought to remain loyal to the Jewish heritage. When this delicate balance was struck one sees the successful synthesis of Judaism and Hellenism.

While each of the expressions of hellenistic piety surveyed herein is distinctive, they all reflect the disenchantment and alienation of their time. Each in some way responds to the confusion and excitement generated by the welter of new ideas flooding the hellenistic world. Each shares a sense of community, or *sympatheia*, with the divine, and thus offers an expanded vision of the world. Most importantly, each devalues the material world, shares the same lack of confidence in the institutions of the day, and shows little interest in history.

Predictably, gnosticism radicalized these tendencies, imposing a terrifying rupture between flesh and spirit, and between the world above and the world below. Where the ancient Hebrews had rejoiced in the creation as God's handiwork and the world was seen as the natural home of all human life, the gnostics viewed this world as a mute, chill landscape, founded by accident and devoid of sense. "The starry sky . . . now stared man in the face with the fixed glare of alien power and necessity."[37]

Chapter 3

Institutions: The Spirit Becomes Flesh

No society exists without institutions, and no society may be understood without some grasp of the nature and function of those institutions. Consequently, our study of the New Testament must go beyond its events and deeds to include the constellation of institutions, customs, symbols, and ethos that stands behind that collection of Scriptures. In the New Testament narrative we hear of tax gatherers, soldiers, priests, Levites, scribes, and Pharisees; we discover the temple, synagogues, courts, families, police, and kings. Little is explicitly said about the institutions behind the actors in the New Testament drama because basic knowledge about such things was customarily assumed. And yet one can hardly understand the intent of the authors or the issues debated without some understanding of the role of these institutions in the development of the New Testament itself. We shall thus dedicate this chapter to that end.

The relationship between the myths and institutions of a society is intimate. The institutional framework, with its basis in everyday experience, is necessary for telling, dramatizing, and interpreting the myths. Institutions provide ways for a people to organize life, to regulate their behavior, to defend themselves, to preserve their traditions, and to mark the passage of significant times and ages in personal and corporate life. The shape of an institution may be dictated by its function—e.g., a school to teach the young, a king to order the society, a priesthood to celebrate life's passages. But myths form the soul of a society, inspiring devotion to the institutions and eliciting respect or reverence for them. The myths of a society point beyond everyday experiences to the deeds of its deity, and thus provide a transcendent vision under which institutional life and institutional order may be constructed. In this manner are the lives of the persons in that society given meaning. Thus the myth is to the institution as the spirit of the society is to its flesh, and together the myths and institutions collaborate to tell each new generation what it should know about life and about its religion.

Many, perhaps most, of the institutions of the first century had long and venerable histories. It was through association with those institutions that the people experienced a form of permanence—the institutions were a given, there when they were born and there, they could be sure, long after they had died. The institutional link with a society's past rigidly chained current practices to traditional patterns of worship and conduct. Although thus anchored to the past, institutions still enjoyed a wide range of latitude. For in order to be truly lasting, an institution must not only sustain traditional values but it must be flexible to accommodate the integration of new values as well. Even when unnoticed, institutions are perpetually in change. Whenever chaos threatens the established order, alternative symbol systems challenge a society's primary myths, and the loss of interest in traditional symbols inevitably effects change of some sort. With this follows the questioning of the wise ones of the society and the emergence of new symbols to replace the old. Revolutionary changes occur in spite of often strenuous efforts to preserve the status quo. The resiliency of institutions must need be enormous, so that even though altered they remain viable.[1] In the following pages we shall examine the functions, structure, and adaptability of the two most important institutions for Jewish religious life, as well as two institutions highly significant in the hellenistic world. These four—viz., the temple, the synagogue, the city-state and kingship—formed the primary building blocks which framed the context in which the New Testament took shape.

The Temple

Every first-century Palestinian Jew lived in a space made sacred by Yahweh's presence. The dark, mysterious, unapproachable, awe-ful glory of Yahweh rested in the forbidding, profound silence of the Holy of Holies—the inner sanctum of the temple. It was from this epicenter of sanctity, the Jew believed, that the entire cosmos received its shape.

When later legend bespoke of Zion as the place where Yahweh stood when he created the world, or when later rabbis referred to the temple as the navel of the earth,[2] they were merely reaffirming what the Hebrews had held true since before the time of the prophets. Jerusalem and its heart and soul, the temple, symbolized for Isaiah (seventh century B.C.E.) God's promises to God's people and God's continued presence with them. To Ezekiel was revealed a vision of a new Jerusalem which would rise up after the Exile. Its vitalizing waters would regenerate the earth, replacing the salty sterile waters of the Dead Sea with fresh (and with fish!), nurturing everbearing fruit trees whose leaves would heal the sick (47:1–12).

Haggai, a post-exilic prophet, fired the enthusiasm of the people with a promise of abundant material blessings if the temple were rebuilt (ca. 520–

515 B.C.E.). Jonah, snarled in seaweed and wrapped in darkness in the belly of the "great" fish, comically moans that he will never see the temple again (2:4). We see, therefore, that long before the time of Jesus the temple was at the center of Israel's faith-experience.

Certain noncanonical writings adopt this prophetic preoccupation with the temple and expand its mythology. The Apocrypha and Pseudepigrapha, written mostly in the period "between the Testaments" (ca. 200 B.C.E. to 70 C.E.), as well as the writings of Josephus and Philo, all assign the temple an important if not preeminent place in the religious life of Israel. The symbolism of that place drew its power from cherished beliefs and images: that Yahweh himself ordered the temple's construction and made his dwelling there; that the earthly version of the temple copied the heavenly model; that the temple stood at the center of the world, providing the axis of divine-human intercourse; that the temple would magnetically draw all people to itself in the Last Days; and that the temple ordered all sacred time and space.

Temple's Celestial Model

The temple was the most spectacular building in Jerusalem, or in fact, in all Israel. Standing on an enormous rectangular platform ringed by a retaining wall almost one mile around, its complex could accommodate up to 75,000 pilgrims during the great festivals.[3] The building owed its grandeur and impact on the people, however, more to the myths of Israel than to its imposing architecture. Through the reenactment and rehearsal of the deeds of Yahweh and the mythic recollection of its sacred, even heavenly origins, both the temple and its liturgy were made holy.[4]

Centuries before the beginning of the Common Era, Ezekiel linked the earthly and heavenly temples in a way that was emulated long after. During the Exile he received a vision of an archetypal heavenly temple which would soon replace the devastated temple of Solomon. This restored temple would be home for Yahweh's glory (kabod) on earth and would renew the dying world. First Enoch makes a similar tie between the temple above and the temple below.

First Enoch 6–36, written before 175 B.C.E., offers a grandiose description of the heavenly temple with a floor and ceiling of fire, a canopy of lightning, and a crown of overarching stars. The temple housed a crystal throne from under which flowed a river of fire and on which sat the Great Glory—blinding, brilliant, and awesome. This heavenly model of the temple will one day replace its earthly copy when "a house shall be built [on earth] for the great King of glory" forevermore (91:13).

In the Testament of Levi (also pre-Christian) this visionary upon being transported to heaven tells us, "the angel opened to me the gates of heaven and I saw a heavenly temple, and upon a throne of glory the Most High" (5:1; see also 3:1 and Apocalypse of Abraham, ch. 18). Third Maccabees tells us that the Holy of Holies in Jerusalem's temple copies the heavenly one (2:15).

As early as the time of Isaiah (8th century B.C.E.) the temple was viewed as a replica of its heavenly version. Worship in the temple was seen as a copy of the celestial liturgy as well. We read in Isaiah 6 that from the Jerusalem temple the prophet was transported to the heavenly one, where he heard antiphonal singing, smelled incense, observed movements of the servants and saw the sacrificial altar with smoking, glowing, red hot stones. We see, therefore, that because of its link with the heavens, the dwelling place of the Most High, the temple, its design, liturgy, and priesthood, all worked together to effect holiness.

The temple architecture duplicated the heavenly model; the temple liturgy echoed the praise of the heavenly council of Yahweh, and the priestly service represented God on earth and interceded for the people before heaven. What Eliade says of temples in general is especially apposite in this context. In his own words,

> the sanctity of the temple is proof against all earthly corruption, by virtue of the fact that the architectural plan of the temple is the work of the gods and hence exists in heaven, near the gods. The transcendent models of temples enjoy a spiritual, incorruptible celestial existence. Through the grace of the gods, man attains to the dazzling vision of these models, which he then attempts to reproduce on earth.[5]

Function of the Temple

The temple, Israel's most important institution, mythically defined all space and time. The temple mount, Zion, was called the "navel of the earth" (Jubilees 8:19), the point where creation began, and the place where heaven was linked to earth, and earth to the underworld. Like ripples moving out from a stone thrown into the water, space, it was thought, expands in concentric circles out from the Holy of Holies, defining Israel's sacred borders. Thus space received its sacred character from that holy nucleus, the temple, and all space not in some way related to the temple was viewed as profane.

The temple defined not only the land but also the cosmic order. Josephus, for example found cosmic significance in the temple furnishings and the garments of the high priest. "In fact," he says, "everyone of these objects is intended to recall and represent the universe" (*Antiquities* 3:180). The menorah, the classic seven-branched candlestick, referred to the course of the seven planets (*Antiquities* 3:182). The tunic of the high priest likewise was tied symbolically to the cosmic order. Its colors signified heaven and earth, its ornamental pomegranate design the celestial lights, its bells the heavenly thunder (*Antiquities* 3:184).

Jacob Neusner has well described the boundaries established by the lines radiating from the altar. He says,

> It was these lines of structure which constituted these high and impenetrable frontiers which separated Israel from the Gentiles. Israel, which was holy, ate holy food, reproduced itself in accord with the laws of holiness, and conducted all of its affairs, both affairs of state and business of the table and the bed, in accord with the demands of holiness. So the cult defined holiness. Holiness meant separateness. Separateness meant life. Why? Because outside of the Land, the realm of the holy, lay the domain of death. The lands are unclean. The Land is holy.[6]

The priestly laws integral to temple service thus functioned to mark off the sacred from the profane. They separated the clean and holy from the unclean, the unholy; they separated life generating forces from death dealing powers. Those who lived in Yahweh's presence—by his law or ties—lived in sacred space. Those outside his law dwelt in profane or even demon-infested space. The temple and its laws thus identified the holy people, Israel, setting this people apart from all others; the temple symbolically marked off the land given by and consecrated to Yahweh, distinguishing this land from all others.

Not only did Israel's geography take its sacred character from the potency of the temple symbol, each person's status in the social order was also assigned by the architectural plan of the temple and the temple cult, which was exclusive by nature. Non-Jews were limited to the court of the Gentiles farthest from the altar; next came Jewish women, who were excluded from the court of the Jewish men; Jewish laymen were forbidden to transgress the court of the priests; and the high priest alone was permitted to enter the Holy of Holies. The sick, the maimed and mutilated, the mentally and physically handicapped were excluded from temple worship. These fixed borders, as unfair and arbitrary as they appear to us today, served a valuable function at the time. In setting limits between insiders and outsiders, as well as establishing an order among the insiders, they preserved Israel's sense of identity and purpose.

In the first century the interest in preserving Israel's distinctiveness was a burning issue. The difference between insiders and outsiders was already much more complex than rhetoric would admit. For two centuries before the Common Era at least, Hellenism exerted a powerful influence on Jews, its prestige carried within the very shadow of the temple itself. No matter how pure and adamantly Jewish some people tried to be, fluency in the Greek language became an economic necessity and quickly came to symbolize status. Persons of influence and means in Jerusalem enrolled their sons in the *gymnasium*, the principal conduit of Greek culture and education, which stood in close proximity to the temple itself. Even tractates hostile to the flirtation with Hellenism copied hellenistic models. (For example, 4 Maccabees, which recalls Maccabean resistance to hellenistic imperialism, draws unmistakable parallels between Eleazar, the Jewish martyr, and Socrates, foremost of Greek martyrs.) Children were given Greek names; many graves were marked with Greek inscriptions, and evidence of the influence of Greek architecture abounds.

Through the unremitting pressure exerted by hellenistic culture from within and without and the willing accommodation made to Hellenism by the upper classes, the distinctiveness and exclusive nature of the Jewish religion was steadily altered. Many Jews uncritically embraced certain features of Hellenism, and almost all were influenced to some degree. But reverse eddies opposing change were also set in motion by this tide of Hellenism. Elitist tendencies grew in certain circles to meet this threat. The Dead Sea community was at least in part reactionary, owing its existence to a revulsion at compromises made by the high priest, the symbolic head of all Israel. Although these challenges affected the temple hierarchy, they did not materially change the symbolic value of the temple itself.

Sacred time as well as sacred space was fixed by the service of the temple. In the major temple festivals which coincided with the turning points of the annual cycle, the service of the altar was synchronized with the movements of the heavenly bodies. The fall festivals—the New Year, Day of Atonement, and the Feast of Booths—were originally a single observance marking the beginning of the growing season for barley and wheat and the harvest season for olives and grapes.

New Year in the ancient Near East traditionally was a celebration of the turn of the earth from death to life, from dormancy to activity. Yom Kippur, the Day of Atonement, observed near the end of the dry season during the fall grain planting, was a period of solemn prayer and fasting. Through blood sacrifices for the sins of the people, divine wrath (death) was averted, replaced by Yahweh's promised covenant and his protection of life. (See Ezek. 43:7–9; 48:35b).

The scapegoat mythically cleansed Israel from all impurities which symbolized death and restored to her the purity which was synonymous with life. Only the high priest, liturgically free of all stain, and only on this day, did enter the Holy of Holies—to utter the most holy, ineffable name. In his prayer before Yahweh the high priest traditionally requested an abundant harvest, a sign of Yahweh's regenerative powers.

Only five days later (the 15th of Tishri) Sukkoth, the Feast of Booths, began. The name itself, the Feast of Booths (and its alternate, the Feast of

Ingathering) suggests the social setting of this celebration. Held during the season of the olive harvest and the winepress, Sukkoth marked the time when farmers moved into makeshift shelters (booths) to guard and harvest their crops. Associated with this "ingathering" there was with the Hebrews as with us in America a ritual of thanksgiving.

Falling at the end of harvest and the beginning of planting, this period was the most optimistic of all times—the time when sower and reaper came together. Celebrated with wild, joyous dancing, revelry, sacrifices, singing, eating, and drinking it was the most exuberant of all festivals (see Judg. 21:19–24). Pilgrims came from great distances and in tremendous numbers for the celebration of this joyous feast at the temple. Only later, it is believed, did Sukkoth recall the Exodus wilderness wandering when the Israelites dwelled in temporary shelters.[7]

The two major spring festivals were Passover (*Pesah*) and Pentecost, fifty days later. Like the Feast of Booths, Passover attracted great numbers of pilgrims, perhaps as many as 100,000 annually. The ritualistic slaughtering of the lamb (originally a substitute for the first born), the eating of meat, unleavened bread, and bitter herbs, and the ceremonial taking of wine in groups of ten commemorated the deliverance of the Israelites from Egyptian bondage. The spilling of the blood in sacrifice and dabbing it on the doorpost sacramentally recalled the experience in Egypt when the death angel *passed over* Hebrew houses marked with lamb's blood in order to snatch life from the first born of the Egyptians. It was this tenth "plague" which the Israelites believed triggered their release from slavery.

Passover, however, beginning on the 14th of Nisan, (from which the date of Easter is derived) was also historically associated with the grain harvest. Although the historical associations of Passover with the Exodus were quite strong, this agricultural emphasis remained also. The barley harvest began at Passover, also known as the Feast of Unleavened Bread, and was followed by the wheat harvest which ran until Pentecost—the Feast of Weeks. (See Exod. 23:14–17.) The presentation of the first fruits of the harvest (Exod. 23:19) was an integral part of these celebrations. In the solemn and grateful offering of loaves made from the newly harvested grain, the people celebrated Yahweh's gift of the harvest, proffered thanksgiving, and recited God's great acts which established them in their land (Deut. 26:1–11).

In all of the festivals of seedtime and harvest the service of the altar was synchronized with the rhythms of the year itself. Sharing in these rites the Israelites reaffirmed their place in sacred time, celebrated a world regenerated and reconsecrated, and reexperienced Israel's sacred story. In passing through this order the celebrant became truly human and shared in what was fundamentally real for all time. (Of course, other aspects of the temple service also reflected this link with sacred time. Both Philo and Josephus, for instance, saw in the twelve stone ornaments of the high priest's robe a symbol of the twelve months of the year and a direct tie with the signs of the Zodiac.)[8]

Although we hear of daily sacrifices and the great festivals, little is known of the temple liturgy itself. We know the Psalms were sung antiphonally, but we do not know when and how. We know sacrifices were offered for sin, guilt, burnt, peace, and thank offerings but we know little more. Probably the *Shema* was used but its place in the liturgy is uncertain (the *Shema* comes from Deut. 6:4, "Hear [Hebrew, *Shema*], O Israel: The Lord our God, the Lord is One.") Doubtless, prayers of blessings and benedictions were an important feature of the worship, but again the part they played is unclear. Nevertheless we do know the service of the temple brought many into the realm of the totally sacred as did no other experience or institution. We see, therefore, how the temple cult figured prominently in all of the observances which marked the turning of the year, and thus defined each new era of sacred time.

The Temple and Israel's History

The symbol system associated with the temple, the building, the ritual, and the priests selectively recalled a rich and varied history. Except for a hiatus in the sixth century B.C.E., the temple of Jesus, Paul, and their contemporaries had a continuous history of almost a thousand years. Even the seventy-two-year gap in the sixth century when the temple was in ruins recalled a tragic episode in Israel's history, the Babylonian captivity, which was indelibly etched on Israel's corporate memory. The festivals likewise invoked the memory of the distinctive and formative experiences of Israel's story: the wandering in the wilderness (Booths), the liberation from Egyptian bondage (Passover), the giving of the Land (Pentecost), and the reconsecration of the temple polluted by Antiochus Epiphanes (Hanukkah). Legendary materials recalled how Yahweh interceded directly to frustrate attempts to violate his Holy Place. Second Maccabees 3:7–25 narrates the story of Yahweh's intervention to smite Heliodorus, a Greek commander, bent on plundering the temple treasury. Third Maccabees 1:11 likewise tells how the prayer of the high priest protected the temple from invasion by pagans.

In the Revolt of 66–70 C.E. much Jewish blood was spilled in a futile effort to halt the Roman juggernaut. The hard core resistance in Jerusalem was suicidal, but the symbolic value of the temple, plus the memory of Yahweh's miraculous defense of his dwelling in the Maccabean revolt, may have inspired the Zealots to choose death rather than surrender to the Romans.

Because the temple occupied such an important place in Israel's sacred story, any compromise of its symbolism often provoked a violent reaction. Josephus tells about the explosive response to Herod's ill-advised erection of a golden eagle over the great gate of the temple court. The installation was viewed as a flagrant violation of the commandment forbidding the fabrication of any "graven image." Thus, according to Josephus,

> [Certain] scholars ordered (their disciples) to pull the eagle down, saying that even if there should be some danger of their being doomed to death, still to those about to die for the preservation and safeguarding of their father's way of life the virtue acquired by them in death would seem far more advantageous than the pleasure of living. . . . For it makes death much easier when we court danger for a noble cause (*Antiquities* 17:152–154).

The sacred character of temple symbolism is also evident in the angry response of the Qumran sectarians to its supposed pollution by an unworthy priesthood. The Dead Sea community owed its origin to priests who rebelled against a corrupted temple. The inhabitants of Qumran found the high priesthood of Jonathan Maccabeus repugnant because he compromised his religion "for the sake of riches" (*1 QpHab* 8:9–11). When opposed by the Teacher of Righteousness, the head of the community, Jonathan visited the Teacher's circle of followers on the Day of Atonement and either publicly humiliated or murdered the Teacher. This dastardly deed earned the "wicked priest" and his colleagues the bitter and lasting hatred of the Qumran community.

The sect subsequently condemned the Jerusalem priests for piling up "money and wealth by plundering the peoples" (*1 QpHab* 9:4–7) for brutally and vengefully "hanging men [their enemies] alive on the tree" (*4 QpNah* 1:7), and called the punishment justly deserved which the Jerusalem establishment received during the Roman invasion of 63 B.C.E. The Qumran community claimed that its priesthood, unlike that of the "wicked priest," was pure and undefiled, keeping itself in readiness for the Day of the Lord. On that Day, they believed, a purified cult would once again be installed by the sectarians in place of that currently in Jerusalem.

In the New Testament, as well as the Qumran Scrolls, both negative and positive responses to the temple attest to the evocative power of this symbol. Luke's Gospel opens in the temple with the dramatic announcement to the priest Zechariah that Elisabeth, his wife, also of priestly lineage, was to have a son (John the Baptist, the forerunner of Jesus). Later Joseph and Mary travel to Jerusalem to present the infant Jesus "to the Lord" (2:22), an obvious allusion to the temple. Again when he is twelve his parents take Jesus to the temple, presumably for his initiation into adult society (2:41–46). At the end of the Gospel Luke takes the reader full circle back to the temple for Jesus' symbolic cleansing and his daily teaching (19:47).

Even after his death and resurrection the church continues steadfastly in temple worship (24:53), and from Jerusalem, the city hallowed by the temple, the church launches its mission. Acts reports that Paul received a vision while praying in the temple (22:17–21). In the Apostle's letters also, the temple metaphor informed his understanding of the church (1 Cor. 3:16–17), of the human body (1 Cor. 6:19), and of Christian sacrifice (Rom. 12:1). The Jerusalem of the End Time, so the Apocalypse tells us, will need no temple because the presence of the Lord and the Lamb will substitute for the temple (Rev. 21:22). In the fourth Gospel, the great temple festivals, Hanukkah (John 10:22), Passover (6:4), Booths (especially 7:37–39), and one other unnamed specifically (5:1) become instruments in the hand of the Evangelist as witness to Jesus who himself is replacement for the temple.

Negative reactions to the temple and its leadership also frequently appear in the New Testament. The Gospels carry the prediction of the destruction of the temple (Mark 13:2; and parallels, Matt. 24:2; Luke 21:6), the stormy cleansing of the temple (Mark 11:15–17), and the angry debates with the temple authorities (Mark 14:53–65; John 18:19–24, et al.). According to Acts Paul was accused of defiling the temple (21:28), a charge which led to his arrest and trial. This is hardly the place to debate the historical accuracy of these heated exchanges. What is certain, and requires emphasis here, is that the temple evoked such extreme positions either of defense or opposition precisely because of its high symbolic value.

Floyd V. Filson, distinguished American New Testament scholar, once said, "The Temple was never an adequate expression of the religious life of Israel. . . . [The] centralization of worship [in the Temple] in the time of Josiah . . . left an empty place in the life of the people."[9] But as we have noted, Filson's popular view is inaccurate. The temple in the time of Jesus and Paul until its destruction in 70 C.E. was clearly the most important institution in Israel. It defined Israel's identity against the nations, gave Israel a language of liturgy, tied her to the cosmic order, anchored the structures of her society, dramatized her history, preserved the Torah, and symbolized Yahweh's presence, and as such offered consolation and hope. If the temple were an *inadequate* expression of Israel's religious life, what else could be said to be more adequate! The expectation of its second rebuilding helped keep the Jewish people as a nation in dispersion, and until this day, Jews from around the world have daily gathered in solemn prayer at its western wall, the last standing remnant from this once proud holy place.

In light of this discussion it is easy to see why the Jewish resistance against Rome made its last stand in the temple, and why through the centuries, from the conquest of Islam to the Christian crusades, and even into the modern era, the region hallowed by the memory of the temple continues to be a powerful force in three great religious traditions: Judaism, Christianity, and Islam.

The Synagogue, Form and Function

The synagogue assumes a prominent place in the New Testament. The Gospel record of Jesus' ministry is punctuated with visits to the synagogue. Luke opens Jesus' ministry with a sermon in the synagogue in Nazareth (4:16–21). In Mark we hear of Jesus preaching and healing in the synagogue in Capernaum (1:21). In Acts Luke leaves the impression that the synagogue was central to the mission of Paul to the Gentiles; for it was only after being rebuffed by his Jewish brothers in the synagogue that Paul would turn his energies to the conversion of the Gentiles. While such a picture contrasts with that in Paul's letters, the fact that the synagogue was formative in Paul's thinking is unquestionably correct.

Much of Paul's early training was probably in the Diaspora synagogue of his parents in Tarsus. His intimate acquaintance with the Greek version of the Old Testament, the Septuagint, presumably came from synagogue meetings or synagogue school. Although Paul rarely explicitly mentions this institution, clearly his relationship with the synagogue continued after his apostolic call. He recalls receiving from the Jews "forty lashes less one" five times, a form of synagogue discipline (2 Cor. 11:24). Many of the questions put to him by Jewish objectors throughout Romans echo synagogue resistance. Though a believer in Christ Paul remains a Pharisee, and as such his association with the synagogue continued.

The Search for Synagogue Origins

Although the synagogue was a vital force in the Hebrew religion of the first century, our information about its origin, worship, and social and cultural activities is sketchy. Inscriptions from third-century B.C.E. Egypt refer to a "house of prayer" (*proseuche*), and archeological data from Greece (Delos) suggest a first-century synagogue there. But the archeological evidence for first-century synagogues is sparse indeed.[10] Professor Yadin, an Israeli archeologist recently deceased, found what he believed to be the remains of synagogues from the time of Herod the Great (34–4 B.C.E.) at Masada, located on the Dead Sea, and at Herodium near Bethlehem,[11] but his conclusions have been disputed.

Literary evidence about the synagogue is more complete. Josephus and Philo, both first-century Jewish writers, speak of weekly meetings of the people. Such meetings or gatherings were most likely called synagogues (from Greek for "brought together"). The place or building where such a gathering took place was at that time also called the synagogue. Josephus refers to a "synagogue of the Jews" in Jerusalem (*Antiquities* 19:300) and to a synagogue in Caesarea (*Jewish War* 2:285). Philo likewise presupposes a gathering on the sabbath when the Jews in Alexandria gave "their time to the one sole object of philosophy with a view to the improvement of character and submission to the scrutiny of conscience" (*On the Creation* 128; see also *The Life of Moses* 2:215).[12] Philo further notes:

> The Jews every seventh day occupy themselves with the philosophy of their fathers, dedicating that time to the acquiring of knowledge and the study of the truths of nature. For what are our places of prayer (*proseukteria*) throughout the cities but schools of prudence and courage and temperance and justice and also of piety, holiness, and every virtue by which duties to God and men are . . . performed? (*The Life of Moses* 2:216).

These sources and the New Testament itself prove that the synagogue was a firmly established institution in the first century. Whether the author of Acts aims to recall historical fact or has other intentions, the synagogue was nuclear to his treatment of Judaism: "For from early generations Moses has had in every city those who preach him, for he is read every sabbath in the synagogues" (15:21). In spite of these allusions to the existence of first-century synagogues, the *origin* of the synagogue remains hidden in obscurity.

Later Rabbis believed Moses created the synagogue. Although historically impossible, such a conviction shows the importance of the synagogue to these teachers of the second and third centuries. Older scholars assigned the synagogue's genesis to the Babylonian exile (587–537 B.C.E.) where it compensated for the loss of the temple. No literary or archeological evidence exists for that view, however. The earliest place of gathering, the *proseuche*, probably originated in the Diaspora, possibly in Egypt, and spread to other lands. Before the Maccabean War (168–165 B.C.E.) Judea was small enough to be served by the temple and its clergy, the priests and Levites. During the expansion of Israel's territory after this war the Hebraic versions of the synagogue spread to outlying areas, especially into Galilee. Consequently, by the time of Jesus synagogues were common in this province at least.

The Pharisaic interest in educating people in the Torah possibly encouraged the diversification of the synagogue. Anything more about the origin of the synagogue would be speculation. Whatever its origin and position in the earlier period, however, by the first century the position of the synagogue was secure throughout Israel, and by the eighties Luke assumed synagogues were a regular feature of Jewish communities of the Diaspora in Antioch, Pisidia, Iconium, Thessalonica, Beroea, Athens, and Corinth. While *full* development of the synagogue does not come until after the destruction of the temple in 70 C.E.,[13] the synagogue we see in the New Testament already provides a powerful social setting for studying the Torah, for prayer, for homilies and instruction, and for providing the people with guidance and consolation in their daily struggles and their search for salvation.

Synagogue Worship

Our knowledge of the structure of the service on the sabbath before 70 is also scanty. There were readings from Scripture, including both Torah (Pentateuch) and the prophets. There were prayers, although the form and content of those prayers was profoundly altered by the destruction of the temple in 70 C.E. and by the growing animus against groups viewed as heretical, such as the Christians. In any case, the Eighteen Benedictions which became a regular feature of synagogue worship, including the curse on the "minim" (heretics), was a later intrusion.[14] Whether some of these benedictions were used in the synagogue prior to the destruction of the temple is unclear, but it is safe to presume that prayers were a regular feature of synagogue gatherings.

A benediction which runs "Blessed art Thou, O Lord our God, King of the Universe who givest us the bread of the field" (or some other gift or deed) appeared early in synagogue liturgy and may be preserved in certain prayers in the Pauline letters such as "Blessed be the God and Father of our Lord Jesus Christ, the Father of mercies and God of all consolation, who consoles us in our every affliction . . ." (2 Cor. 1:3f.; see also Rom. 9:5b). Doxologies and prayers of thanksgiving seem also to be echoed in Romans 6:17; Romans 11:36; 1 Corinthians 15:57; 2 Corinthians 8:16; 9:15; and Galatians 1:5. Not only on the sabbath but also on feast days many faithful unable to make the pilgrimage to Jerusalem celebrated in the synagogue instead. After 70 and the destruction of the temple we see the transfer and integration of many of the temple rites into the synagogue liturgy. This transmission assured the survival of these rites, but it effected great change in synagogue worship as well, making reconstruction of the earlier liturgical order even harder.

Scholars often impose the order of service found in late rabbinic materials on the synagogue worship of Jesus' day, but such a practice is anachronistic.[15] In the Diaspora the formal worship in other religions may have influenced the services in the synagogue. Nevertheless even in Israel it is more likely that the worship, like the buildings, still varied greatly from place to place. The nonclerical or lay character of the synagogue community would tend to support this view. Irrespective of the form of the worship, though, certain aspects of the institutional life of the synagogue are clear.

The synagogue, both in Israel and in the Diaspora, was a vital community center. In addition to worship the building, however plain, often served as a hostel for Jewish travelers, a dining hall, a school, a place for the administration of community discipline or justice, and an assembly point for the elders. Social and political purposes were also served by the synagogue. Doubtless the synagogue, like the church in colonial America, served as a gathering place for immigrants who from the sixth century B.C.E. on were often the victims of uprooting, deportations, and resettlement programs. At weddings, funerals, and feasts the synagogue was the institution which eased transitions and offered a convenient gathering place for ritualizing those occasions. It provided an organization where a Jewish minority could organize to lobby for their interests with local magistrates or Roman officials. It was the place where Israel's sacred story could be retold and mythically reexperienced again and again.

In a setting where the majority culture threatened to assimilate or drastically alter the Jewish religion, boundaries were necessary for the preservation of identity. With the insistence on monotheism, the reinforcement of the laws of purity, and the regular rehearsal of the traditions Diaspora Jews were able to maintain their identity. However, hellenistic influence remained strong. Accommodations were made, but the synagogue was *the* institution providing the practical setting and symbolic power to establish effective fences against "pagan" influence. The dilemma created by these competing claims is captured by Luke's portrait of Paul as a Roman citizen, son of Jewish parents, resident of Tarsus, whose speech was Greek but whose soul remained Jewish, who skillfully used both the Stoic diatribe and rabbinic methods of argumentation and who had learned from both Greek philosophers and Jewish rabbis.

The synagogue, then, had a multiple function—religious, social, and political. After the destruction of the temple the synagogue filled a large portion of the void. Its religious function tended to predominate, and thus it came to be known as a "holy place," assuming some of the aura of the temple itself. Thus when Jesus went to the synagogue on the sabbath, this gathering was important *for him* as well as for the community. Enough flexibility existed in the service, however, to allow Jesus, a layman, to read and interpret the Scriptures (Isa. 61:1–2 in Luke 4:18–19), even though he was not trained as a rabbi. Luke's account of this event also underscores the importance of the place for Jesus' dramatic pronouncement. The vigorous participation of Jesus in synagogue life is thoroughly evident in the Gospels.

Many of these synagogue narratives in the Gospels speak of conflict between Jesus and those who stand for the prevailing religious ethos. Jesus, we are told, teaches in the synagogue with authority (Mark 1:22, 27), whereas the scribes are presented as lacking such authority. But the Gospels also indicate that Jesus' authority was challenged in the synagogues. Jesus offers a novel interpretation of Scripture which angers his synagogue audience (Luke 4:24–29). He is hampered by the unbelief of folk from his home town when he preaches in the synagogue in Nazareth (Mark 6:6). His sabbath healing in the synagogue triggers designs on his life for breaking the law (Mark 3:1–6). And in Mark 13:9 we find allusions to synagogue beatings (or scourges) for followers of Jesus. Elsewhere Jesus castigates religious pretension (Mark 12:38–40) and hypocrisy (Matt. 6:2) practiced in the synagogue.

Although Jesus' own preaching and teaching were doubtless provocative and critical of the prevailing symbol system, this criticism was intramural. He was in no way rejecting Judaism, its Scriptures, and institutions. Instead his was a disruption caused by the proclamation of a Jewish gospel of the kingdom of God by a Jew to other Jews. The gospel he preached of the arriving kingdom generated stresses and strains in the synagogue itself, but the narratives as preserved in the Gospels (especially Matthew) carried a different message to the post-seventy church. These stories were selected, arranged, and interpreted by the Gospel writers to reflect the growing tensions between the synagogue and the church in this later period. In Matthew the quarrels had reached the bitter, name-calling stage, and in the fourth Gospel the clashes were so severe that a divorce between the synagogue and the church was taking place. Thus the fact that these clashes were staged by the Gospel writers in the synagogue, a highly strategic institution, not only reflects the historical situation but also underscores the historical relationship of Christians to this institution as well.

Synagogue Leadership

Every institution has its action (myths, rites, liturgy, etc.) and its actors. Although the synagogue was primarily a lay institution, certain persons were nonetheless authorized to explain the rules of the community and to preside over their observance; others were empowered to define the terms of life in the community and to enforce those definitions. Although there was no priestly hierarchy in the synagogue some leaders are recognizable. (Priests probably could and did participate in the synagogue activities, but they occupied no position of privilege or place.) A helpful insight into the nature of synagogue leadership is offered by an inscription found in Jerusalem in 1913–14.

The text refers to an early synagogue in the Holy City and to leaders and patrons of the synagogue. The inscription names Theodotos (thus the *Theodotian* inscription), an *Archisynagogos* or head of the synagogue whose father and grandfather had also been *Archisynagogoi*. This inscription shows the head of the synagogue not only enjoyed a position of respect and authority, but also remained in that position indefinitely as a sort of patron of the synagogue. Ofttimes the contribution of the *Archisynagogos* toward the construction and maintenance of a building or program was critical. In the Theodotian inscription we learn the synagogue in question was built by the fathers of Theodotos and the elders with the help of one Simonides.[16]

The Gospels also name certain synagogue officers. Mark mentions by name a certain Jairus, one of the "rulers of the synagogue," who sought Jesus' help for his mortally ill daughter (5:22). Luke refers to a "ruler of the synagogue" critical of Jesus for healing on the sabbath (13:14). This honorary head of the synagogue was sometimes assisted by an attendant or deputy (*huperetes*) and apparently a council of elders. In Luke 4:20, for example, after Jesus had read from Isaiah, he handed the scroll to the deputy (*huperetes*). Josephus mentions the "archon of the Antiochene Jews" (*Jewish War* 7:47) which probably refers to the "head of the council of elders," a central body with representatives from different synagogues in such large cities as Alexandria and Antioch.[17]

The organization of the synagogue was simple and varied from place to place. The duties of the lay functionaries were administrative, not clerical, for no ordained clergy directed synagogue life. These lay officials handled necessary arrangements for services on the sabbath and feast days, assisted with housing for travelers, managed the building if there were one (synagogues were often held in homes), took care of the scrolls, and possibly also presided at services and meetings of the synagogue. Aside from the references to these officials we know almost nothing about the social structure of the synagogue itself in the time of Jesus. Because the congregation and lay officials were responsible for the synagogue, though, this omission is entirely understandable.

The New Testament mentions certain synagogue patterns which were taken over into the church. Some official similar to the deputy or head of the synagogue is mentioned in 1 Thessalonians 5:12 where Paul encouraged respect for those who "work among you, and those in authority over you in the Lord, and those instructing you" (author's translation). As with many synagogue congregations, the early churches met in homes. Their activities, also like those of the synagogue, included sabbath gatherings, prayers, instructions, almsgiving, readings from the Scriptures, and homilies, as well as resolutions of conflict and the provision of housing for travelers. The church, like the synagogue, also maintained internal discipline (Luke 12:11 and 1 Cor. 6:1–4) and took pains to mark itself off from the world.

The Diaspora synagogue was an institution open to all persons—pious Greeks interested in the Jewish religion, women, and children. (Whether women and children were segregated or what role they played in the assembly is disputed.) Accessible as well as open, the synagogue differed from the temple in Jerusalem where the *shekinah*—the presence of God—was believed to dwell, and where priests offered daily sacrifices according to the ancient rites of Israel. Although the Torah prescribed regular trips to the temple, such pilgrimages were not always possible. Because of its accessibility the development of the synagogue was revolutionary. Easily available throughout Israel and the Diaspora, the synagogue offered a setting for the weekly invocation of God's blessing and guidance and for the observance of the Jewish rites; it was the organizing center for the teaching of customs indispensible to the preservation of Israel's identity; it was the arena for telling the stories and enacting the myths central to Israel's consciousness as a people. Although there was no rivalry between the synagogue and the temple, the synagogue offered a form of lay participation, guidance, and accessibility unknown through the temple religion.

The Greek Polis

Within two decades after the death of Jesus we learn of a vigorous Gentile mission to Greek city-states. Inevitably the ambience of the *polis*, one of the oldest and most influential institutions in the Greek experience, left its mark on both the missionaries and their converts. When the Greeks expelled the Persians from Athens in 510 B.C.E. the way was opened to the development of the independent city-state. For a time democracy prospered, individual expression was encouraged, and a period of unparalleled artistic and intellectual achievement flourished.

With the defeat of an alliance of Greek cities by Philip of Macedon in 338 B.C.E. and the later conquests of Alexander, however, some believe this classical period or "golden age" ended and the less illustrious hellenistic era began. Certainly after the death of Alexander in 323 the Greek cities slid into a decline never fully reversed. Nevertheless, for centuries the cities retained some of the allure and excitement of the classical age. Sculpture from the classical period still revealed the beauty and vitality of that glorious past. Centuries old architectural masterpieces still bore witness to the Greek genius (and some do so still!). Even under monarchy some democratic institutions remained, weakened to be sure, but still supportive of individual creativity and artistic expression. The free inquiry which served as the basis for the golden age of philosophy survived—though in a confused and discouraged state. The temples of the gods still testified to the once-sacred presence which consecrated the city. Theaters remained active. *Stadia* still opened to games, harbors to commerce, and the citizens' assembly (*ecclesia*) to free discussion and debate.

Though citizenship was limited and precious, the cities welcomed aliens (*metics*) providing they had a citizen sponsor. The *metics* had no political rights, could not own house or land, paid high taxes when citizens paid none, performed military and public service; and yet they came because of the opportunities the city provided. They brought fresh ideas, new ways, beneficial skills, and an eagerness to work—all valuable commodities for the city in need of economic stimulation and constant renewal. Besides the *met-*

ics, several times as many slaves swelled the population of the city. Around 300 B.C.E. Athens was said to have 21,000 citizens, 10,000 *metics*, and 400,000 slaves. Even if a quarter the estimate the number of slaves was still large.

Many slaves were talented, educated persons who by reason of poverty or war had fallen into bondage. Their presence, although involuntary, also contributed mightily to the intellectual and artistic life of the city-state. Thus this pluralistic unit integral to the social and political life of the Greek culture was suffused with a hybrid mythology containing both Greek and foreign elements.

The ritual associated with the Olympic games served to keep the ancient myths fresh; transplanted agricultural myths from Egypt and Asia Minor blossomed in the mystery religions of the cities. Far into the Roman period the hellenistic myths of divine origin, of divine presence, and of divine benefaction enlivened the cities. Even though monarchy stripped the cities of their political autonomy they remained vibrant centers of mythic interaction and expression.

Though subjugation under Alexander had undermined the autonomy of the cities, both he and his successors did tend to leave control of internal affairs to local authority. Cities could collect taxes, mint coins, maintain courts, administer police, encourage trade, establish markets, develop harbors. Benefactors for municipal projects—the theater, libraries, baths, and temples—were constantly being sought. The *ecclesia* served as a forum for discussing community concerns and for voting honors on such benefactors.

While the freedom to conduct domestic affairs remained in the hands of the cities, though, the power to raise armies, to organize navies, and to conduct foreign affairs were reserved for the territorial rulers alone. Thus obviously the health and vitality of the city was directly dependent on the good will and benevolence of the potentate. That good will was often lacking so that the cities often slipped into decline, or occasionally, organized leagues of cities for defense. Clubs sprang up, draining off energies once given to the city. Philosophies increasingly cynical about the value of public institutions focused more and more on the individual. Finally this decline of the cities caused many to look elsewhere.

Alexander established few cities. His successors, however, short on manpower needed to control such vast territories, established Greek cities as instruments of public policy. Thirty are known in Palestine alone. Some were old Phoenician cities converted into Greek cities (e.g., Tyre, Sidon, Beirut, Gaza); some were new cities which straddled trade routes (e.g., Pella in modern Jordan on the caravan route); some were cities which voluntarily organized themselves as a Greek city (e.g., Jerusalem by 175 B.C.E.!).

Economic decline in Greece and the prospect of a fresh start with citizenship in a newly established hellenistic city led to mass immigrations to Asia Minor, to Palestine, and to a lesser extent to northern Egypt. These new cities provided a pool of manpower for the army, skilled artisans for the city, and centers of commerce and industry for each region. They also formed a platform for displaying the hellenistic culture to great advantage. Asia Minor and the eastern territories were made up of vastly diverse peoples and cultures. This vast network of hellenistic cities with their common Greek culture and Greek language helped to stabilize a territory in constant danger of fragmentation. The impact on the native populations is well illustrated by the story in the Gospel of Mark about the Greek woman, "a Syrophoenician by birth," who came to Jesus seeking help for her sick daughter (7:24–30).

It was this urban setting with its common language, its spirit of ecumenism, its willingness to experiment, its accessibility by both land and sea, its concentrations of people, its spiritual ferment, its competing myths and its interaction with other cities that formed the setting—some would say the perfect setting—for Paul's mission. Some before him and others after concentrated their proselytizing in the cities. Apparently, though, none were as successful as Paul in understanding the urban culture, nor as adept as he in exploiting the opportunities it provided for preaching his gospel.[18]

Hellenistic Kingship

Kingship was native to the Middle East. The cities of Sumer in lower Mesopotamia had kings in the third millennium B.C.E. The pyramids serving as royal tombs witness to the presence of kings in Egypt as early as 2800 B.C.E. The small kingdoms in Palestine like Edom and Moab had kings already when they break into view in the Old Testament. Even Israel after some initial resistance followed her neighbors, embracing kingship around 1000 B.C.E.

Later the Greeks left democracy for a monarchy, and from the time of Alexander the Great until the Roman period kings governed throughout the hellenistic world. Even when the hellenistic kingdoms gave way to Roman rule in the second and first centuries B.C.E., Greek ways continued though in altered form. Since the policies of these kings and the mythology supporting kingship bore so heavily on the destiny of their subject peoples, informing so fully the religious language and outlook of the Greco-Roman world, some treatment of them is desirable.

From the dawn of recorded history to the Roman era myths treating the intimate relationship between the kings and the gods abound. A Sumerian king like Gilgamesh, even if partly divine, was yet a mortal moving inexorably towards death. His annual union with a temple priestess ceremonially reenacted the renewal of the cosmos thus emphasizing his sacral function, but he remained subordinate to the gods, chosen by them but never their equal.

By contrast, the Egyptian king, known as pharaoh, appeared as very god incarnate, immortal, and invincible. He reigned not in stead of Horus but as Horus himself, son of Ra, lord of the two lands, king of upper and lower Egypt. He secured the cosmic rhythm, assured health and peace, and "drove out disorder from the Two Lands so that order was again established in its place."[19] Head of the society and equal to the gods, pharaoh integrated the social and cosmic orders, served as the ceremonial head of the cult, the chief of the bureaucracy, and the center of the Egyptian religion. Remaining intact throughout the Persian rule to the time of Alexander, this Egyptian mythology was in an ideal position to influence the hellenistic view of kingship.

Early Hebrew traditions, on the other hand, scrupulously separated divine rule from the human, resisting any and all pressures to deify the king. The first commandment allowed no confusion of the king with Yahweh. Given the significance of religion among the Hebrew people, however, some connection between Yahweh and the king was inevitable. David brought the ark to Jerusalem; Solomon built the temple. Isaiah 11 tied divine deliverance to kingship, and a late tradition in Zechariah 12:8 spoke of Yahweh's future rule when "the house of David shall be *like* God, like the angel of the Lord" (emphasis added). Unlike the Egyptian and Sumerian views of kingship, though, the kings in Israel did not integrate society and nature, nor community and cosmos, and the Hebrew view of Yahweh's austere transcendence prevented the complete identification of the king with God. Although the attempt to design Israel's kingship after the hellenistic model occasionally enjoyed some success, it also met fierce resistance.

Though democracy was the ideal in classical Greece it did not always function well in the city-state. Vulnerable to despots and mobs, lacking the discipline of its totalitarian neighbors (e.g., Sparta), and suffering from debilitating rivalries with other cities, the democracy in the city-state gradually gave way to monarchy. Long before the time of Alexander, Herodotus, a Greek historian, expressed his preference for a virtuous king as the ideal governor (ca. 480–424). Similarly, Socrates (b. ca. 469) and Aristotle (b. 384) saw the philosopher-king as the best means of regulating society. Many pious folk held the king equal to the gods and therefore entitled to govern; others unable to revere the king as god nevertheless believed the monarch to be at least god-like, hence on a plane quite different from the ordinary. Esphantus, a Pythagorean philosopher from the late fifth century B.C.E., ranked the king above his subjects, "a copy of the higher king . . . a single and unique creation" (*Stobaeus* I, vi, 19). This superior status made him a model worthy of imitation and an object of popular worship.[20]

While Greek thought in the classical period was more self-contained, Alexander's conquests opened the way to a synthesis of eastern and western traditions. Alexander's rule of Egypt entitled him to be recognized as the god Horus. While we cannot be sure if he sought to exploit the Egyptian deification, this Egyptian myth of the divine king at least confirmed trends already set in motion before Alexander. The blend of traditions emphasized the right of divine mandate, if not the divine status of the king himself, and thus titles like savior (*sōtēr*), and the eponyms of god (*epiphanes*), benefactor (*euergetes*), and lord (*kurios*) also confirmed the king's divine status.

In the Roman period, the attitude of the emperor toward the hellenistic ruler cult ranged from outright rejection to enthusiastic endorsement. Augustus Caesar (27 B.C.E.—14 C.E.) discouraged divine ascriptions from his countrymen but accepted them from elsewhere for political reasons. From Pergamum on the western coast of Asia Minor came an inscription honoring him as "The Emperor, Caesar, son of God, the god Augustus, of every land and sea the Overseer."[21] In 24 B.C.E. an Egyptian swore an oath "by Caesar, god of god," an entirely appropriate act in the Egyptian setting.[22] Over their objections both Tiberias (14–37 C.E.) and Claudius (41–54 C.E.) were called "lord" and "savior." The list could be lengthened considerably.

Some emperors broke with the tradition of claiming divine titles and prescribing participation in the imperial cult as a test of loyalty to the state. Gaius (37–41 C.E.), though, nicknamed Caligula because of the high military boots he wore as a young boy, actively solicited divine honors, encouraged temple building in his honor, struck coins depicting himself as sun god, and claimed to speak with Jupiter as a personal friend.[23] Such a public identification with the gods may have disgusted Jews, but was not resisted. When Alexandrian Greeks tried to force Jews to display an image of Gaius in the synagogue, however, violence erupted.

A delegation of Jews from Alexandria led by Philo sought Gaius' assurance that Jewish rights would be protected. Jews were willing, Philo says, to honor the Emperor as "Savior and Benefactor," but their religion did not permit them to worship the emperor or to set up his image in the synagogues. Evidently the delegation enjoyed some success, but another incident in Palestine pushed the Jews to the brink of open revolt.

Responding to anti-Jewish sentiment in Jamnia, a coastal city west of Jerusalem, Jews destroyed an altar erected to Gaius. The Emperor was predictably insulted and in reprisal ordered the erection of a mammoth bronze statue of himself in the temple at Jerusalem. Only the personal intercession of the Jewish King Agrippa in 40 and the threat of massive Jewish resistance led Caligula to recant.

While Nero sought to use the Christians as a scapegoat to blame for the fire in Rome in 64 C.E. which he was suspected of setting, it was Domitian

(81–96 C.E.) who first sought to force Christian observance of the imperial cult. Coins proclaimed Domitian "father of the gods," and he required those seeking an audience to address him as "our lord and god." He made participation in the imperial cult mandatory and used the observance as an acid test to identify "enemies of the state."

Under Trajan, Domitian's successor, the persecution continued. A letter to the Emperor from a Roman legate dispatched to an Eastern province in order to investigate Christian resistance reports as follows:

> this is the course that I have adopted in the case of those brought before me as Christians. I ask them if they are Christians. If they admit it I repeat the question a second and third time, threatening capital punishment; if they persist I sentence them to death. . . . All who denied that they were or had been Christians I considered should be discharged, because they called upon the gods at my dictation and did reverence, with incense and wine, to your image which I had ordered to be brought forward for this purpose . . . and especially because they cursed Christ, a thing which, it is said, genuine Christians cannot be ordered to do.[24]

Most scholars believe that the persecution under Trajan was an extension of the savage treatment of Christians under Domitian, and that the book of Revelation was written to support the suffering church. Revelation 13:15 speaks of those slain because they refused to worship the beast of the sea, and 17:1, 6 refers to Babylon, a code name for Rome, as "the great harlot" who is "drunk with the blood . . . of the martyrs of Jesus." The acclamation of Jesus, as "King of kings and Lord of lords" (19:16) as well as the sharp contrast of the "Lord Christ" and "Lord Caesar" throughout the book protests the absolute claims of the imperial cult and draws precise boundaries between the Christian church and the dominant culture.[25]

The influence of the ruler cult on the church was hardly confined to these episodic outbreaks of persecution; it provided a whole constellation of images and symbols which the young church appropriated to describe its leader. We noted above how the predicates "lord," "benefactor," "savior," "manifestation of god," and "god" attached to the king. Some of these acclamations devoted to the king surely were appropriated by the church to praise Jesus. That *kurios* (lord), for example, was widely used as an everyday term to refer to the emperor was surely known to the church (see Acts 25:26). Not surprisingly, in Philippians 2:9–11 Paul quotes an early Christian hymn which acclaims Jesus as Lord in a style reminiscent of the praises lifted before the emperors: "Therefore God has highly exalted him and bestowed on him the name which is above every name that at the name of Jesus every knee should bow in heaven and on earth and under the earth and every tongue confess that *Jesus Christ is Lord*" (emphasis added). In Mark 11:9 both royal imagery and *kurios*-language unite in the acclamation, "Hosanna! Blessed be he who comes in the *name of the Lord*! Blessed be the kingdom of our father David that is coming!"

The titles *savior* and *benefactor* are synonymous terms going back to the hellenistic era when *savior* was used to praise human deliverers—physicians, military commanders, and kings.[26] Somewhat immodestly Josephus tells us the Galileans called him "savior and benefactor." Although the phrase appears infrequently in the New Testament (24 times), it carries a powerful message. In Luke's birth narrative the angel announces Jesus' arrival: "to you is born this day in the city of David a Savior" (2:11; see also Acts 13:23). John 4:42 has the Samaritan woman hail Jesus as "the Savior of the world." Whatever its origin, the term *savior* in the New Testament preserves a hellenistic nuance. The word sets Jesus apart from the ordinary and clearly designates him as the conveyor of salvation.[27]

The New Testament use of the term *king* doubtlessly owes something to Israel's special history and eschatological hope. The identification of Jesus as son of David secures his place as a king (see Mark 10:47; 11:10; 12:35; Matt. 1:1; Rom. 1:3, et al.), but this Jewish understanding was hardly insulated from the hellenistic views of kingship in the Greco-Roman world. In the New Testament we view the merging of these traditions.

These four institutions, the temple, the synagogue, the *polis*, and kingship definitively shaped the early Christian consciousness. The Gospel writers almost casually speak of the preeminent place the temple and its functionaries held in first-century Jewish life and their import for the memory of the early church. For others—like Paul, the author of Hebrews and the visionary behind the book of Revelation—the temple carried high symbolic value.

Even though relationships were strained, the Jewish community with its synagogue was home for the "Messianists," or Christians, until after the destruction of Jerusalem in 70 C.E. Even when the conversation turned rancorous, as in the Gospels of Matthew (85 C.E.) and John (95 C.E.), the ugly exchanges still emphasize the importance of the synagogue as a powerful though threatening presence.

The resourceful exploitation of the *polis* and its rich cosmopolitan heritage accounts at least in part for the success of the early Gentile mission. And finally, both for better and for worse, the Middle Eastern mythology of kingship contributed to the church's self-understanding. In opposition to the imperial cult (see Revelation) the church defined its own boundaries. And drawing on a royal mythology as old as the Middle East itself, the community framed its beliefs about Jesus, forged its hymns to God, and fashioned a language appropriate to its status as a messianic community.

Chapter 4

Scripture and Interpretation

At death, during periods of historical terror, at a dream's collapse, or the fracturing of a religious symbol, as well as in singular moments of high joy—the birth of a child, a wedding, the embrace of a new age—the human family has always groped for language adequate to express its inner stirrings, its pain or joy, its hope or despair. In the Judaeo-Christian experience, that language has often come from the Scriptures. Just as Blake called the Old and New Testament "the Great Code of Art," so the Old Testament and other Jewish Scriptures form the Great Code for the New Testament. On virtually every page quotations, metaphors, or symbolism from the Hebrew tradition rise up to grab the reader's attention. Paul alone quotes the Old Testament ninety-three times and alludes to those Scriptures even more. Jesus likewise found proof in the sacred texts for the arriving kingdom and content for his message.

An awareness of the way texts were read and the symbolic power they have had will help us better understand the New Testament itself. As important as is a grasp of the way in which the language of the Scriptures was incorporated into Christian writings, though, such an understanding is hardly enough. It is necessary also to know the mechanics of interpretation—for example, the manner in which the texts were manipulated sheds insight into how those texts were understood. To that purpose, then, we devote this chapter.

The Scriptures were central to the thought and life of every first-century Jewish community. They defined social roles, provided a moral code, offered instruction and comfort, and informed the symbol systems of relevant institutions. Weekly readings in the synagogues recalled Israel's story and mythically revived her experience with Yahweh. Knowledge of the Scriptures conferred status. The sage was deemed wise, not merely because he was insightful and profound, but more importantly because he was learned in the Scriptures. Although these texts were unfailingly experienced as sacred they in no sense constituted a static tradition, for as we shall see, to the first-century interpreters the Scriptures were ever alive with mystery and surprise. These interpreters of holy texts felt free to improvise, edit, combine, select, and adapt texts (and variants of texts) in order to release their secrets. Thus, although the texts were experienced as holy, they were not fixed. Both in their selection and interpretation the exegetes enjoyed enormous freedom.

The situation was made even more fluid by the absence of clear limits of what was scriptural (i.e., canonical). The bounds of the canon were not marked clearly until near the end of the second century C.E. Consequently, the spectrum of sacred writings was broad and comprehensive. Among the Dead Sea Scrolls were represented not only every book of the Hebrew Bible except Esther, but also such non-canonical texts as Enoch, 2 Baruch, the Genesis Apocryphon, and numerous other works. As we shall see below, the scope of the traditions was expansive and the interpretation of the texts was ingenious within a diverse Judaism and emerging church.

The Text to Be Interpreted: The Septuagint

Since the writings of the early church were written in Greek for Greek speaking congregations, one would expect that their Scriptures would be in Greek as well. At least two centuries before the time of Jesus the Hebrew Bible was translated into Greek because the Jews of the Diaspora no longer understood Hebrew. The Letter of Aristeas[1] recounts the legend behind the translation.

King Ptolemy II Philadelphus (284–247 B.C.E.), so the tale went, lacking a copy of the Torah for the library in Alexandria, brought seventy-two scribes from Jerusalem to render the Hebrew Scriptures into Greek. In seventy days, according to a later legend, the scholars, working independently, made translations which agreed in every single detail. The Greek translation, called the Septuagint (from the Greek for seventy, thus LXX), originally contained only the Pentateuch, but in later centuries was expanded to include the prophets and writings as well (i.e., Psalms, Proverbs, Job, etc.).

Understandably, this translation which was read and discussed in the synagogues, memorized and studied in the schools, and interpreted by the pious exerted an enormous influence on the Judaism of the Diaspora. Although the quality of the translation is uneven (the Pentateuch being rather reliable, Samuel and Ecclesiastes woodenly literal, and Job and Proverbs more like a paraphrase than a translation), efforts were made to preserve in the LXX the spirit of the Hebrew text. Nevertheless it was inevitable that the Greek idiom, once adopted, would change the nuance, miss the subtlety, and even alter the meaning of the Hebrew text. At the same time the Greek version of the

Scriptures created its own idiom much as did the translation of the Bible authorized by King James in 1611.

Many Diaspora Jews were intensely hellenized; to them the anthropomorphisms of the Hebrew text (i.e., suggestions that God acted in a human way) were highly offensive. The translation provided an opportunity to remove such embarrassing images. In the LXX, therefore, such texts were sometimes altered.[2] In addition enigmas were solved and crudities softened. For instance, for the Hebrew of Exodus 15:3, "Yahweh is a man of war" (author's translation), the Septuagint substitutes, "The LORD is the one who annihilates wars" (author's translation).

In this text the Septuagint makes three significant changes. It substitutes the Greek term *Lord* (*kurios*) for the ineffable Hebrew name, Yahweh; it omits the reference to Yahweh as "a man" (Hebrew, *ish*), and it completely reverses the meaning of the text to say God causes wars to cease rather than initiating them. We see therefore in this Greek translation a strong aversion to the view that God contends like a human. The translation thus not only avoids an anthropomorphism but also makes a moral judgment, i.e., that war is evil. Another text makes a similar change. For the Hebrew of Numbers 12:8, "he [Moses] shall see the form of Yahweh," the LXX has "he [Moses] *saw the glory* of the Lord (*kurios*)."

In the Greek translation efforts abound to solve certain enigmas of the Hebrew text which have puzzled interpreters for centuries. The Hebrew version of Exodus 4:24, for example, makes the troubling suggestion that when Moses was returning to Egypt from his father-in-law's house (along with his wife and child) Yahweh challenged him "at the lodging place" and "sought to kill him." The translators took exception to the bizarre suggestion that Yahweh would capriciously murder any person, much less Moses, so the text was smoothed to say, "And it happened on the way, in the inn, that an *angel of the* LORD [not Yahweh himself] met him and sought to kill him" (emphasis added).

In response to this threat, according to the Hebrew text, Moses' wife, Zipporah, circumcised the child and touched Moses' feet (a euphemism for the groin) with the blood in order to offer Moses magical protection. In the Septuagint the euphemistic reference to the groin is completely missing. Instead Zipporah "fell at his [the angel's] feet," apparently to beg safe passage from the agent of death. At these and other points we see how the translators interpreted or even altered the Hebrew text to reflect their own religious outlook. While the importance of such fine points may elude the nonspecialist, they nevertheless illustrate the dynamic nature of the interpretive task and the freedom the ancients felt to alter the sacred writings.

Tolerance of other worldviews was integral to Hellenism but historically alien to the Hebrew religion. At points the Septuagint reflects that universal outlook. Even when not subscribing to all forms of religious piety the Septuagint urges respect for them. One Hebrew word for God, *Elohim*, takes a plural form. When *Elohim* is used to allude to Israel's God, it unfailingly refers to the one God of Israel. Thus the Hebrew text of Exodus 22:28, "You shall not revile Elohim" means proper honor must be accorded Israel's Lord. But, given the respect for all religious traditions in Hellenism, the Hebrew word for God, Elohim, is taken as a plural and given quite a different meaning: "you shall not revile *the gods*" (emphasis added).

Though the change may strike the reader as insignificant it had major implications for the Hebrew tradition which revered one God to the exclusion of all others. It encouraged an openness and tolerance of all religions which was quite alien to the Hebrew Scriptures. Although Paul in particular subscribed to the rigorous monotheism of the mother faith, his hellenized converts in Corinth saw no harm in attending the worship of the gods (see 1 Cor. 10:14–22). The reading from the Septuagint above would support this practice.

The trend toward abstraction is higher in hellenistic piety than it is in Hebraic. This tendency appears in Exodus 3:14 where instead of Elohim's ambiguous revelation of the holy name, "I am who I am. . . . Say this to the people of Israel 'I AM has sent me. . . .'" the Septuagint has "I am *the being (ho ōn)*. . . . Say to the children *the being* has sent me" (emphasis added). In this translation of the Septuagint Yahweh is depicted as absolute being—the cosmic, divine substance of the Greek philosophers.

Although numerous other alterations were made, these examples are sufficient to show how the hellenistic spirit informed the translation of the Septuagint. While the insinuation of these Greek views into the translation did not materially alter the fundamental nature of the Hebraic religion, it would be inaccurate to say no change in outlook occurred. An awareness of Septuagintal tendencies is important for two reasons: (1) the Septuagint was the Bible of many Jews throughout the Greco-Roman world, including most of the early church; (2) the freedom to reinterpret and even modify the text to coax meaning from it for each successive age was enjoyed not only by these translators but by the New Testament writers as well.[3] The LXX left a rich legacy. It was in Paul's blood; its style was imitated by Luke, and its texts vitally influenced the early church's language and outlook.

Philo of Alexandria

A consideration of Philo (15 B.C.E.—ca., 45 C.E.) is important not only because he was a contemporary of Paul and Jesus (though he was known to neither) but also because he was a prolific writer, giving us perhaps our best view of first-century hellenistic Judaism. Since he contradicts himself occasionally one might wonder if he accurately represents the worldview of Diaspora Judaism. Allowing for his unique mannerisms, though (which are considerable), the substance of his views agrees with that of the Septuagint.

Without question Philo was a cosmopolitan thinker, well versed in the major Greek philosophies of his time—Platonism, Stoicism, and Neo-Pythagoreanism. He drew on the works of Homer and Hesiod for his own work. Even though thoroughly hellenized, Philo was deeply committed to the Jewish traditions, institutions, and welfare. He wrote to deliver his Jewish compatriots from an oppressive sense of inferiority that came from living in the shadow of a pervasive, powerful, and alluring hellenistic culture. Turning the tables he sought to show that Judaism was superior to Hellenism— that Plato took his great insights from Moses and that the Hebrew Scriptures were both compatible with and superior to Hellenism. Philo was a master of appropriating the insights, methods, and language of the Greeks to vindicate and rationalize the traditions of Judaism; yet Scripture, rather than hellenistic philosophy, was surely the controlling force in Philo's thought.[4]

Philo's hermeneutics (from the Greek *hermeneia*, meaning interpretation) calls for our special attention. He is best known for his expert use of allegory to interpret sacred texts. Using this tool of the Stoics, Philo rationalized anthropomorphisms, deciphered riddles, and spiritualized the mythic images of the Septuagint. He hoped thereby to articulate the higher law in Torah and to elicit the deeper meaning of Israel's festivals and institutions.

Believing the literal meaning of a text contained only its superficial intent, Philo openly shows his contempt for literalists. He calls them "slow witted" (On *Flight and Finding* 179; On *Dreams* I, 39), "obstinate," "rigid," and "resentful" (On *Dreams* II, 301). He ridicules them as apostates who trivialize or reject the truth of the Scriptures (On *the Confusion of Tongues*, II, 6–8; On *Husbandry* 157). Only through allegory, he believes, can the deeper meaning which underlies the literal be evoked.

A sample of Philo's allegories will illustrate his method. His use of allegory to soften anthropomorphisms appears in his treatment of Genesis 2:8. A literal reading of the report that Yahweh planted a garden of "soulless" plants struck Philo as silly. The reference, Philo argues, was not to literal plants but to God's endowment of the world with soul and reason. Such divine gifts (plants) bear the fruit of virtue, insight, and the wisdom to distinguish between the beautiful and the ugly (On *the Creation* 154). Similarly, since no biologist knows of a "tree of life," Philo takes this allusion to refer symbolically to "reverence toward God . . . by means of which the soul attains to immortality [i.e., life]" (On *the Creation* 154).

Whenever a text contradicts common sense or known facts Philo searches for its secret or hidden significance with his technique of allegory. Psalm 46:4 speaks of "a river whose streams make glad the *city of God*, the holy habitation of the Most High." Since Philo assumes the reference to the "city of God" meant Jerusalem and since it was common knowledge that no river flowed through the holy city, then the text if taken literally was in error. Philo concludes, however, that the Psalmist wrote "to show us allegorically something different from the obvious" (*On Dreams* II, 246). He argues that the river must refer to the "impetuous rush" of the divine *Logos* (word or reason), the "delight, the sweetening, the exhilaration, the merriment, the ambrosian drug . . . whose medicine gives joy and gladness" (*On Dreams* II, 247, 249).

Scripture tells us about an ass which talked to Balaam his owner. Again Philo uses allegory to decipher the speech of this talking donkey. According to Philo the donkey's words refer to an unspeakable language which judges Balaam the master for his slowness to learn: "it is not your life-pursuits which bring your share in good or ill, but the divine reason" which teaches patience in adversity (*On the Cherubim* 36). Here Philo's method is informed by an overriding moral concern as well as a desire to understand a problem passage.

Elsewhere Philo employs allegory to bridge the gulf between the work's context and his own. The Exodus narrative, he contends, speaks not just of the liberation of the Israelites from Egyptian bondage but also to his contemporaries in Alexandria. Moses, he offers, "led *us* forth" out of Egypt, that is "out of *our* bodily passions" (emphasis added). Philo compares Marah, the bitter water from the desert spring, with the sensual appetites which bewitch "*us* with their haunting music" (emphasis added).

The readiness of the children of Israel to return to captivity to escape the rigors of the desert speaks of the perennial human tendency to surrender freedom's struggle for the safe but "dissolute and licentious life" of captivity. The destruction of the golden calf in the wilderness witnesses to the need for the "lover of virtue" to burn up "the pleasures of the body." (*The Posterity of Exile of Cain* 155–159). While Philo's denial of the body and pleasure is more Greek than Hebraic and his spiritualization of texts may strike us as arbitrary, his approach nevertheless remained faithful to the nucleus of the Hebrew Religion—that is, it retained a concern for the God of the first commandment as the center of all faith and morality.

Of particular interest is Philo's allegorical treatment of the two creation stories in Genesis 1:1—2:4a and 2:4b–25 and the narrative of Sarah and Hagar. In the creation stories he juxtaposes the heavenly man of 1:1—2:4a created in the image of God with the earthly man of 2:4bff. made from clay. The heavenly man who was divine by nature needs no commandments; the earthly man on the other hand needs the limitation and guidance provided by the commandments. The second Adam therefore, rather than the first, was forbidden to taste the fruit of the tree of knowledge. The heavenly man, Philo says, was inherently wise, perfect, and virtuous. The earthly man by contrast tended toward error, disobedience, and immaturity thus requiring the fences provided by prohibitions (*Allegorical Interpretation* I, xxx, 94–95; see also I, xii, 31).

A similar split possibly underlies Paul's contrast of the first and last Adam (Rom. 5:1–12 and 1 Cor. 15:47–50). The Apostle, however, reverses the chronological sequence we see in Philo, placing the earthly Adam first, and the heavenly Adam last. The first he equates with the Adam of both Genesis stories; the role of the last or heavenly Adam is filled by Messiah Jesus. Paul concludes from this construction that just as the entire human family shares in the destiny of the first Adam (mortality and death), through faith all may share in the destiny of the last Adam (salvation and life). Thus while the application is entirely different in Paul the typology resembles that known to Philo and perhaps widely shared in hellenistic Judaism.[5]

Philo, like the Greeks, thought of mathematics, rhetoric, music, and mythology as studies preliminary to gaining wisdom—to being a philosopher. In the story of Sarah and Hagar he found evidence to support this notion of education. The reader will recall that Sarah, thinking she was barren, suggested that Abraham seek children through her servant, Hagar. After Hagar gave birth to Ishmael, Sarah in a fit of jealousy ordered Abraham to evict the Egyptian slave and her son. Later Sarah and Abraham have a child of their own. Ignoring Hagar's dispossession Philo suggests that Abraham's relationship with Hagar, like the preparatory studies in the gymnasium, was preliminary to the full possession of wisdom symbolized in his union with Sarah.[6]

Although Paul's allegorical interpretation of the Sarah-and-Hagar story is quite different, it may be informed by an understanding similar to Philo's. Paul contrasts the two, likening Hagar to the Israel of old and Sarah to the church. Paul like Philo, however, accords Hagar and the Israel devoted to the law a preparatory function. Certainly Paul shared with Philo, and perhaps the Judaism of the day, an appreciation of the evocative character of this story as well as the belief that allegory could release its hidden meaning. Differences between the two authors were pronounced, however. Unlike Philo's pervasive use of allegory, Paul's hermeneutical explorations were considerably more restrained.[7]

The Interpretation of Scripture at Qumran

Geza Vermes, a respected British scholar, makes a simple but important observation about ancient Judaism: in ancient Judaism, he notes, "systematic theology was unknown, and the establishment, transmission, and development of doctrines and beliefs were effected within the framework of scriptural interpretation."[8] Of no group is this observation more apt than of the Qumran community. This community appealed to the sacred texts to validate its truth, to authorize its discipline, and to guarantee its future. At the heart of the community's worship, mission, and hope stood the Scriptures. As central as those holy writings were, however, still they were no static entity. Traditional methods of interpretation and teaching were adopted from the Judaism of the day and adapted to the new situation. Sometimes old views were fractured to allow the mysteries concealed in Scripture to spring forth.

Integral to the interpretation at Qumran was the belief that the community was living in the last days. This eschatological reading of Scripture assumed the secrets (Hebrew, *razin*) of holy writ hidden from all ages were first revealed to the Teacher of Righteousness, the community's founder, and then to the community. These secrets, so it was thought, were revealed *only* to the sectarians who studied and meditated on their contents literally in shifts night and day; and these secrets offered guidance for the living of the final days. Philo, too, we might recall, interpreted the Scripture to address his own time, but the eschatological preoccupation of the Qumran community plays no important role in Philo. Allegory, so central to Philo, held only a peripheral interest for the Dead Sea community. Conversely, the commentaries on Scripture which the community wrote are missing altogether in Philo's writings. The approach of each though starkly different in approach and outlook can help us better understand the way New Testament authors worked with texts.

In ancient Israel sacred traditions were routinely reinterpreted in light of new economic, political, and social factors. The commandments found in Exodus, for example, were amplified in Deuteronomy. Job and the author of Isaiah 40—55 modified the Deuteronomic presupposition that suffering was punishment for sin and prosperity a reward for good deeds. The story of Israel's emergence found in 1 and 2 Samuel and 1 and 2 Kings was completely recast in Chronicles. This procedure which was followed throughout Israel's history provided a vital link between ancient message and new circumstance. We need not be surprised, therefore, when the Scrolls (and the New Testament) offer radical scriptural interpretations.

Most of the manuscripts at Qumran deal with the preservation, interpretation, or imitation of the sacred tradition.[9] Although all of the "books" of the Hebrew Bible except Esther appear in the Qumran collection, it is anachronistic to speak of the "Bible" of this period. Since no canon or rule existed for assigning scriptural status, the line between sacred and profane texts was fuzzy. We see at Qumran, for example, a tradition including not only the law, the prophets, and the writings of the Hebrew Bible, but also such "books" as Ecclesiasticus, Tobit, Jubilees, Enoch, the Testaments of Levi and Naphtali, all appearing in the Apocrypha and Pseudepigrapha. In addition commentaries exist on portions of Genesis, Deuteronomy, and Samuel, as well as on the prophets Isaiah, Ezekiel, Hosea, Micah, Habakkuk, Nahum, Zephaniah, and selected portions of the Psalms, Job, and Daniel.[10] From this vast collection we learn how the community interpreted its sacred texts.

Commentaries on Scripture

The most common form of scriptural interpretation in the Qumran Scrolls is the *pesher*, from the Hebrew for interpretation. The *pesherim* (plural) treat texts thought to conceal mysteries which grudgingly surrender their secrets only to the gifted religious figure through divine revelation. These commentaries which favor certain prophetic books (e.g., Habakkuk, Isaiah, Hosea, Micah, Nahum, and Zephaniah) all follow a typical format.

First they cite a small portion of a text, offering a commentary on a key word or phrase in the text having relevance for the community. The Qumran commentary on Habakkuk 2:2 illustrates this procedure. In the primary position stands the text itself: "AND YAHWEH ANSWERED [AND SAID TO ME (i.e., Habakkuk)]: WRITE DOWN THE VISION AND MAKE IT PLAIN UPON THE TABLETS SO THAT HE MAY READ IT EASILY [THAT READS IT]." The interpretation follows: "And God told Habakkuk to write down the things which will come to pass in the last generation, but the consummation of time He made not known to him [i.e., Habakkuk]. And as for that which He said, THAT HE MAY READ IT EASILY THAT READS IT, the explanation (*pesher*) of this concerns the Teacher of Righteousness to whom God made known all the Mysteries (*razin*) of the words of the Prophets" (1 *QpHab* VI:14—VII:4).

We see therefore how the sectarians believed a mystery revealed to a prophet in the sixth century B.C.E. remained obscure to all until it was divined by the Teacher of Righteousness in the second century B.C.E. Hence an ancient text, through inspired exegesis, received contemporary relevance. The theological interests of the Community sometimes dictated changes in the text to "improve" its meaning.

An instance of rather creative interpretation appears in the Qumran treatment of Habakkuk 1:5. The Hebrew text reads: "LOOK AMONG THE NATIONS [*BAGGOYIM*], AND SEE; WONDER AND BE ASTOUNDED." F. F. Bruce noticed the sectarians changed *baggoyim* (nations) to *bogedim* (traitors) thus radically altering the original meaning of the text. Through this change the text acquired another focus. "Look among the traitors" was substituted for "Look among the nations" and was interpreted to refer to the "evil priest" responsible for the martyrdom of the Teacher of Righteousness.[11] In this instance we see how a text, though viewed as sacred, lost none of its plasticity. In the first century the canons of interpretation allowed (and expected) the alteration of the text itself to give voice to basic religious convictions.[12]

Since the charter of the elect community came from the Scriptures, not only sacred texts but also biblical allusions were thought to mirror the community's destiny. Habakkuk 1:5, for example, describes the devastation inflicted on the forests and wild life by the Babylonian invasion in the late seventh and early sixth centuries B.C.E. Citing the prophet's invitation to view this destruction "FOR THE VIOLENCE DONE TO LEBANON WILL OVERWHELM YOU, AND THE CRUELTY USED AGAINST THE BEASTS WILL TERRIFY YOU. . . ." the community then adds: "The explanation of this word concerns the Wicked Priest inasmuch as he will be paid his reward for what he has done to the Poor [i.e., the Qumraners]; for LEBANON is the Council of the Community, and THE BEASTS are the simple of Judah who practise the Law" (1 QpHab XI:17—XII:5). Whereas the prophet used the word LEBANON to refer to northern Israel, and later Jewish interpreters used LEBANON as a code word for the temple[13], here the term is invoked to allude to the community, a replacement for the temple.

That the sacred texts were predictive by nature was a central conviction of the community. The prophetic demand of Malachi to bar persons from sacrificing old, sick animals in the temple was interpreted at Qumran to predict the separation of the sect from the "sons of the Pit" and thus closing the door to participation in the temple cult (CD VI:11–15). Centuries earlier Amos had forecast exile "beyond Damascus" for an idolatrous people who worshiped Kaiwan, the star god, and served under Sakkuth, the king. The sectarians took the reference to "the land of Damascus" to predict the exile of the community on the Dead Sea in the "land of Damascus." The reference to "Sakkuth, the king" was changed to "sukkath [booth] of the king" and read as a reference to the Congregation at Qumran. Thus a prediction of doom by Amos became a forecast of the special place the community (booth) was to have in the divine story (CD VII:15–16).

Midrash as Interpretation[14]

Midrash, from the Hebrew darash meaning to seek, search out, or inquire, is a form of imaginative interpretation which seeks the inner meaning of biblical narrative for teaching purposes. Some midrash treated ethical concerns (Halachah) while other midrash was more didactic or explanatory in nature (Haggadah). The Genesis Apocryphon known only through the Dead Sea Scrolls surely qualifies as Haggadah.

This fragmentary document retells the early Genesis story, interspersing the old text with fresh interpretation. In this expanded version of the original, for example, we are given in graphic detail a full account of a passing reference in the biblical text to Sarah's beauty (see Gen. 12:11–16). From the midrashic expansion we hear the sectarians exclaim, "[How] beautiful is the shape of her countenance!" We learn that her shape, hair, nose, eyes, face, breasts, arms, and hands were all the quintessence of beauty. Her long, graceful fingers, her beautiful legs were captivating. From the description it is no wonder the Pharaoh was completely smitten by her and plotted to take her from Abraham. From this vivid, full and artful description of Sarah we see a full appreciation for human beauty among the sectarians. We see, therefore, they were not as bloodless as sometimes thought.

A word of caution is in order here, though. Among the purposes of the midrash entertainment was surely included. The supplements often attempt to solve problems lodged within the text itself. We are not told, for example, in the biblical narrative how Abraham knew that the Pharaoh would seek to kill him. In the Genesis Apocryphon we learn that he was warned in a dream.

Imitations of Scripture

The Hymn Scroll contains songs of thanksgiving and praise that imitate the structure, language, and themes of the canonical Psalms. Opening with "I give thanks, O Adonai" or "Blessed be Thou," many of the hymns swell with gratitude for God's mercy and deeds of salvation. Other hymns contain confessions, laments, and other moving expressions of a soul in search after the manner of the Psalms. Although all of the hymns are assigned to the Teacher of Righteousness it is unlikely that he wrote all or even most of them. Whatever their source, they reflect the most cherished views and deepest existential concerns of the community itself. They doubtless brought reassurance, comfort, and encouragement to the waiting, beseiged community.

Arranged in a soaring, poetic style, these hymns capture many of the themes of the canonical Psalms, e.g., the majesty of the creation—and add others of their own, such as the bitter struggle between the "children of light" and the "children of darkness," the tender mercy of the Creator for his faithful "poor," and the revelation of the divine mysteries to the elect.

In spite of their keen awareness of the ugly face of evil, the sect, like the Psalmist, saw the fingerprints of the Creator in creation itself. From those traces of divine work the community took encouragement for their struggle:

> It is Thou who has spread out the heavens for Thy glory
> [and] hast [created] all [their hosts] according to Thy will
> together with the mighty winds according
> to the laws which governed them . . .
> the stars according to the paths [which they follow]
> [the clouds of the rain] according to the office which they fulfill,
> the thunderbolt and lightnings according to the service appointed unto
> them. . . .
> It is Thou who has created the earth by Thy strength,
> the seas and the deeps [and the rivers]. . . .

[And Thou has cast a lot] for the spirit of man which Thou hast formed in the
   world
for everlasting days and unending generations to ru[le over the works of Thy
   hands];
[and] Thou hast allotted their service unto them. . . .
      1 QH 1:9–16

Note especially the final paragraph and the link it forges between the
creation and the service of the redeemed.

Composite Quotations

Texts strung together like beads appear in the New Testament with some
frequency (see especially Rom. 3:10–18). Before the discovery of the Scrolls
scholars wondered if such clusters were unique to the New Testament. After
the Qumran discovery, however, all doubt was removed. Texts also were
arranged there in tandem, linked by a common motif. In the manuscript, 4
Q Testimonia, a cluster of texts supports the messianic expectations of the
community. Deuteronomy 5:28–29 is linked with Deuteronomy 18:18–19,
predicting the advent of a prophet supreme like Moses who, so it was
thought, would appear in the final days. These texts in turn were joined to
Numbers 24:17 referring to the Star of Jacob and the Sceptre of Israel—or as
the sectaries believed, to the royal Messiah; then came Deuteronomy 33:8–
11 and the allusion to the priestly Messiah.

In this series of texts the Qumran interpreters found evidence for the
appearance of three eschatological figures—a prophet, a priestly Messiah,
and a kingly Messiah. The final link in the chain was formed by Joshua 6:26,
a non-canonical text from the Psalms or Joshua which berated the "wicked"
adversaries in Jerusalem. Although this catena of texts offers a literary precedent for the New Testament composite quotations the correspondence is
scarcely exact. Each citation in the Scroll collection is distinctly longer than
any found in New Testament *testimonia*. The literary precedent offered by
Qumran, however, is valuable in that it shows such composite quotations
were a recognized feature of scriptural interpretation of first-century Judaism.

Allegory

As noted above, Philo made copious use of allegory in his interpretation
of Scripture. The Qumraners also used allegory, though in a more limited
sense. The Damascus Document (*CD*), for example, cites Numbers 21:18,
a song about water in the desert placed on the lips of the wandering Israelites:
"Spring up, O well!—Sing to it!—the well which the princes dug. . . ." The
sect, however, allegorized the allusion to the well to refer to the law and the
origins of the community. Let us listen to the words of the document itself:

The well is the law,
And those who dug it are the converts of Israel
who went out from the land of Judah
and were exiled in the land of Damascus,
all of whom God called princes . . ."

In sum, we can see how the Qumran community used Scripture creatively to seek authority for their doctrines and discipline, to predict the future they envisioned, to mark boundaries between themselves and the "sons of Darkness," and to create the form of their liturgy. We have observed their use of the commentary on Scripture (*pesher*), their imitation of Scripture (e.g., Psalms), their expansion of Scripture (Midrash), their arrangement of texts in clusters, and their use of allegory.

In both content and approach we see in the Scrolls many parallels to the New Testament itself. Although the community viewed both the origins and future of the congregation in light of the sacred traditions, we can hardly assume a self-conscious construction of principles of Scriptural interpretation and their systematic application. There is of course a great difference between using methods of interpretation and being aware one is employing such methods. Although the Qumran sectarians did not do the latter, in early rabbinic interpretive guides we do see a self-conscious development.

The similarity between New Testament and Qumran interpretation is clear. Both believe the ancient texts conceal forecasts of the last days which can be discovered with the proper inspiration. Both view the prophetic books as integral to the eschatological vision of the community (e.g., Mark 1:2–3). Both range outside the canonical Scriptures to find support for their views (e.g., Luke 11:49; 1 Cor. 2:9; James 4:5). Both use allegory, albeit sparingly (Mark 4:14–20). Both reinterpret or even alter texts to reflect the new situation (e.g., Rom. 1:17). Both radicalize the Torah (Matt. 5:19–30). Both arrange texts thematically (Rom. 3:10–18; 9:33; Matt. 2:1,5; 21:42, et al.). Finally, both use one text to interpret another (Rom. 4:3–8). Both use texts to prove they are the true people of God (Rom. 9:25–26). Both use Midrash (1 Cor. 10), and both imitate the style and form of the sacred texts (note the septuagintal style of Luke 1:68–79; 2:29–32, et al.).

Although these parallels are impressive, disparities do exist. The mixing of citations, quite common to the New Testament (e.g., Rom. 11:8 is equivalent to Deut. 29:3 and Isa. 29:10; Rom. 11:26 is equivalent to Isa. 59:20 and Isa. 27:9; Mark 1:2–3 is equivalent to Mal. 3:1 and Isa. 40:3) is skimpy if not absent from the Qumran Scrolls. Both use prophetic texts, but the selections vary and the interpretation of each is rather different. The *pesher* method so common at Qumran appears infrequently in the New Testament (see Acts 2:14–24 on Joel 2:28–32). The underlying secrets of Scripture are revealed in one case through the Teacher of Righteousness and in the other through Jesus of Nazareth. Clearly in both, Scripture was used for apologetic reasons, although with a very different slant. In the case of Qumran it was employed to reinforce the belief this community was the elect of Israel. The New Testament apologetic focuses more directly on the Messiahship of Jesus in light of his death and resurrection.[15] Such a comparison shows how New Testament interpretation reflects the hermeneutics of the time and differs from accepted practice.

Rabbinic Interpretation

Since the compilation of rabbinic materials occurred near the end of the second century C.E. and later, it is hazardous to construct a model of rabbinic exegesis for the pre-seventy period from them. Yet Vermes is correct in that those who focus exclusively on the Qumran materials miss the contribution made by the broader spectrum of Jewish interpretation. The rabbinic materials are significant for New Testament study even though the separation of early traditions from late ones is enormously complex. While granting Vermes' point that one should view the New Testament in the context of all of the Jewish writings of the day (including the Apocrypha and Pseudepigrapha), because of their late date the rabbinic materials must be used with great caution.[16]

Seven rules of interpretation are commonly assigned to Hillel, a distinguished rabbi whose life overlapped the time of Jesus (60 B.C.E.—20 C.E.). David Daube taught us some of Hillel's rules may go back to the early Greek philosophers, and were adopted and modified by the early rabbis to reflect their own concerns.[17] It is instructive here to examine selectively some of Hillel's rules and compare them with selective patterns of interpretation in the New Testament.

The first of Hillel's rules, Hebrew *Qal Wahomer*—the light and the heavy—draws weighty conclusions from less weighty premises. For instance, the rabbis read Exodus 20:25 to allow the construction of an altar of stone, or brick, or any other materials. Since the altar was the most sacred fixture of the temple and could be built of any material, the rabbis reasoned other less important temple objects could likewise be constructed of any available material. The reasoning by analogy could move in either direction: from the heavy to the light (as in this case) or from the light to the heavy.

This rule probably informed the discussion in Matthew 12:9–12 and Romans 5:15–21. The Gospel passage raises the question about healing on the sabbath. According to Matthew Jesus asks "What man of you, if he has one sheep [of lesser value] and it falls into a pit on the sabbath, will not lay hold of it and lift it out?" Of course, the implied answer is: "No one! For the law so permits." Then the analogy is drawn: "Of how much more value is a man than a sheep!" The implication is clear. Moving from the less to the more weighty case, Jesus argues that healing on the sabbath is lawful.

Similarly, in response to Jewish skepticism about how one man's faithfulness can redound to others, in Romans Paul shows first how one person's destiny (namely Adam's) affected the destiny of many. Beginning with the weaker example (Adam), Paul recalls how many are partners with Adam through his act of disobedience. Just so, Paul argues from the lesser to the greater, may many participate in the act of obedience of the second Adam, Jesus, through faith in him as the Messiah.

The second rule, *Gezerah Shawah*, seeks to understand a passage by drawing analogies through link words found in other passages. For example, Hillel reportedly decided it was legal to sacrifice a Passover lamb even though the Day of Preparation (the day for the slaughter) came on a sabbath and even though the law nowhere explicitly permits such action. Hillel solved the dilemma through analogy from link words. Numbers 28:2 states that the *daily* sacrifice (*tamid*) must be made *at its appointed time* (*bemoado*). From Numbers 28:9 we learn that this rule applies even if the "appointed time" comes on a sabbath. Numbers 9:3 on the other hand required that the Passover sacrifice (*pascha*) be offered "at its appointed time" (*bemoado*), but no reference to the sabbath is made. By analogy, Hillel reasoned, since the use of *bemoado*, "at its appointed time," applied when the daily sacrifice fell on the sabbath, the command to offer the Passover sacrifice *bemoado*, "at its appointed time," implied that this offering must be made as well even when the time appointed fell on the sabbath.

Paul's discussion of the relevance of Abraham's example for his own day is similarly established. In Romans 4:1–12 Paul begins his discussion by quoting Genesis 15:6: "Abraham believed God, and it was *reckoned* to him as righteousness" (Rom. 4:3, emphasis added). Since the promise comes before Abraham is said to obey any commandment (i.e., circumcision), Paul reasons that the reckoning of Abraham's righteousness was due to God's grace and not observance of the law. This generosity is viewed by Paul in light of Psalms 32:2f, where forgiveness of sin (or grace) is taken to mean that "the Lord will not *reckon* [count] his sin" (my translation). Paul then, reasoning by analogy, draws the conclusion that just as Abraham was *reckoned* righteous because of faith or grace rather than works, so also Gentiles who believe in God for his work in Christ will be *reckoned* as righteous without the law (4:22–23). Although the content of Paul's argument belongs to his belief in Messiah Jesus, his method is taken from the rabbis (see also Matt. 12:3–6), for in these inner connections between texts established with link words their moment was given meaning.[18]

Hillel's third, fourth, and seventh rules have little bearing on New Testament interpretation. His fifth rule, *Kelal Uperat*, draws normative conclusions from the general to the specific and vice versa. This rule states that in cases where a statute contains inclusive and more restrictive terms, it is always the one in the final position that dictates the scope of the text. To illustrate Leviticus 1:2 decrees that an offering shall be brought to the Lord "from the beasts (*behemoth*), from the oxen, and from the sheep (or goats)" (author's translation). The more specific references to oxen and sheep appear in the final position and thus are restrictive as to the kind of beasts which may be sacrificed. Only these domestic animals, according to the ordinance, are acceptable. Undomesticated animals—wild beasts such as deer—may be eaten in some cases but they may not be sacrificed. We see therefore how the general category first mentioned—"beasts"—is defined by the later specific references. Exodus 22:7 was read in a similar manner. This text treated the liability of man given custody of a neighbor's ass, oxen, sheep, "or any beast." Unlike the law above, this regulation moves from the specific to the more inclusive category. The all embracing reference to "any beast" in the final position guards against any neighbor limiting his liability to oxen or sheep. So his responsibility is expanded to include any beast over which he is given custody.

A similar pattern may be observed in the parenesis of Romans 12:20–21 where a set of specific, limited instructions is followed by an inclusive one. Paul says, "if your enemy is hungry, feed him; if he is thirsty, give him drink . . ." (quoting Proverbs 25:21–22). Then Paul adds a general exhortation: "Do not be overcome by evil, but overcome evil with good" (Rom. 13:8–9). No one following Paul's guidance would have felt that he had satisfied the requirement of discipleship by merely giving food and drink to the enemy. He must do whatever was necessary to overcome evil with good (see also 1 Cor. 7:29–31). It was the final general admonition that was normative.

The sixth rule of Hillel, *Keyose' bo bemakom 'aher*, prescribes the ways Scripture can be interpreted in light of other Scripture, one text by another. A trait in one text may be illumined by a similar trait in another text (instead of a word as in rule two). The oft mentioned case of Moses holding up his hands to assure success in the battle against Amalek is instructive (Exodus 17:11). One instinctively asks, why did Moses have to keep his hands elevated? The rabbis answered by appealing to Numbers 21:8 where Moses erected a bronze serpent so that all looking on the object might be healed of deadly snake bites. They were healed, the rabbis believed, not because the symbol was magical but because the elevated serpent pointed their vision beyond the symbol to Yahweh above. Similarly, the rabbis argued, Moses' elevated hands directed the attention of the warriors to the source of their help, namely Yahweh (see Rosh haShanah 3:81).

Paul may use this principle of interpretation in Galatians 3. While discussing the promise given to Abraham, Paul quotes Genesis 12:3: "in you shall all the nations be blessed" (Septuagint). In another version of the same account the expression *in you* is changed to *in your seed* [*or offspring*] (Gen. 22:18). After concluding that the phrase *in your seed* refers to *in you*, Paul makes a rather dramatic interpretive leap. Reading *seed* as singular he takes this key word to refer not to Abraham's *many* descendants but to one and one only, namely Christ. Then Paul interprets Genesis 12:3 by way of Genesis 22:18 to mean "in you [i.e., in Christ] shall all the nations [i.e., Gentiles] be blessed" (Gal. 3:8)."[19]

The New Testament writers may not have followed these guides to achieve a high level of consistency, nor may they have consciously applied Hillel's rules of interpretation to the Scriptures. Their hermeneutic, however, certainly does belong in a constellation of Jewish interpretation that includes the rabbinic approach. For though the *codification* of Hillel's rules may have come later, given the early date of hellenistic efforts to decipher textual meaning through reasoned and consistent guidelines it is hardly surprising that similar patterns should surface in the New Testament.

Summary

The mechanics of textual interpretation were so creative and complex only because of the grip that they had on every first-century Jew. The meticulous preparation and preservation of sacred scrolls, the diligent copying of Scripture, and the consuming study of the text all reveal the transcendent quality of the sacred writings. A reverence for each word—each powerful, mysterious, even magical word—was rooted in the belief that the text was the record of God's dealings with the chosen people, God's address through prophets and priests to the community of faith, and God's threats against antagonists. The divine origin of its speech gave the text a numinous quality, and an inexhaustible character. The record of God's dealings with Israel gave the text a historical dimension, and God's promises and prophetic prediction opened the text to the future.

The experience of reading these texts was different from reading other texts because the sacred writings were seen as a repository of wisdom or divine knowledge. Like a puzzle enfolding divine secrets, the sacred text required inspired efforts, special insight, or special techniques to unlock its treasure. To those gaining access, the rewards were abundant. Nothing short of redemption or apprehension of divine truth graced the savant. The interpretive methods served a dual task: (1) they were used to gain entry into the primary world of the sacred text; (2) once admission was gained, they offered a means of releasing the spirit of the letter or of sharing the boon of the sacred treasure with the community.

Of course, the interpreters made no pretense of objective critical study.

They interacted with the text in a closed hermeneutical circle. They viewed the text through their own world, and then in turn viewed their world through the text. A holy figure, a religious symbol, a basic conviction might imbue the text with meaning. Then the text might become the lens through which shared convictions, dominant symbols, and holy figures were viewed. From world to text then back to world again the circle ran. In this active interchange thought was provoked, insight gained, convictions buttressed, and boundaries secured. In this lively engagement with the text the community's language gained a richer texture and meaning, a deeper substance, and a holy framework. Through this active dialogue the text became a vehicle for integrating the community into the sacred. We see, therefore, that the text was never a "thing" to be squeezed for meaning with sterile techniques but a world to be understood, a history to be celebrated, a tradition to be addressed, reverenced, and appropriated.

In the discussion above we have seen how the understanding and interpretation of sacred texts in the Judaism of the day influenced New Testament writers. The belief among all Jewish groups that God's revelation was embedded in the ancient texts and that properly interpreted secrets could be learned and applied to each successive age is securely established by modern scholarship. The interpretation of texts in the bright light of the approaching, final denouement was central to the method of both Qumran and the New Testament.

The use of such texts to authenticate the existence and beliefs of the community was also widely shared. The particular way some texts were interpreted by others was known at Qumran, among the rabbis, and in the New Testament. Moreover, we now know Paul shares with the Qumran interpreters the tendency to arrange texts on a common thread of meaning. The use of Midrash, "typology,"[20] summaries of biblical narrative, and allegory were also widespread in the Jewish exegesis of the day. A shared methodology, however, often produced strikingly different interpretations. For the theological presuppositions of the interpreters directly influenced the way texts were read. In every case, though, it was inconceivable that an authentic form of religious expression could emerge without some relationship to the sacred text. Each community of faith was alive to the text. Thus, the text was experienced as a dynamic reality, revealing the future, enlivening the past, and lending significance to the present.

Chapter 5

Demons and Holy Men

A dramatic struggle unfolds before us in the New Testament. Sinister forces in human form contest Yahweh's claim to the world. Demonic agents clutch their hostages, resisting Jesus' order to free them. A fearsome anti-Christ makes war on Christ's followers. Satan seeks to tempt Jesus from his mission, inflicts illness on the unsuspecting, leads Judas to betray, and seduces new converts to abandon the "way." Malevolent principalities and powers strain for cosmic dominion and the right to dictate all human destiny. While this bizarre scenario may grate against modern sensibilities, in our private and collective dreams, and indeed in episodes like the Holocaust in our common history, these surrealistic nightmares emerge to haunt us as real possibilities. Since the eschatological struggle between demons and angels, Satan and Yahweh, suffused first-century Jewish and Christian thought and is central to much of the New Testament, it will be helpful to examine the shape, scope, and scale of this mythology.[1]

The term *myth* refers not to some patent falsehood, as in its popular usage but to the world of sacred story ritualistically enacted which is inhabited by a people firmly planted in the realm of the really real. As such, myth deals less with what happens historically than with the profundity of what happens, less with literal truth than with the experiencing of that truth in the historical unfolding of tragedy in the natural world. Thus myth which survives as poetic narrative has a timeless quality, a reach beyond its own place, a spiritual depth which offers insight into difficult issues, which keeps the sacred past alive, and which opens up new levels of understanding.

As I write these words, Jewish people worldwide are preparing to celebrate Passover. Although many have never traveled outside their national borders, all will affirm, "We were slaves in Egypt." Thus through the mythical reenactment of the Exodus story these modern Jews will become contemporaries in that significant event, will reexperience the liberation of the people of Israel, and will reaffirm their confidence in God's promises.

Black American slaves also mythically appropriated the Exodus experience in the spiritual:

> Go down, Moses,
> Way down in Egypt land,
> Tell old Pharaoh
> Let my people go.

Although the story is about Hebrews enslaved in Egypt in the second millennium B.C.E., it nevertheless became bread for a proud people suffering oppression and yearning for freedom. In this Black spiritual we see the Exodus event mythically transformed to stretch beyond restrictions of time and place. The myth as used here does not repudiate history but revalues it in light of a contemporary experience. The sacred story works because it becomes the story of the people reciting it.

The functions of such mythic experiences are multiple: they order societal and individual worlds threatened with chaos; they construct models for human conduct; they preserve wisdom necessary for self understanding; they provide present consolation and hope for the future; they stimulate reflective thought. As a myth recalls beginnings through a poetic narrative which transcends both poetry and narrative, it places a people in touch with what is fundamentally real for all time. The church has valued the New Testament so highly because it both shares in and witnesses to God's activities in the beginning of a new age, activities which believers claim have meaning for all time.

In the following pages we shall consider a prominent theme of the New Testament—the raging conflict between the cosmic forces of good and evil. Although pain, suffering, and historical tragedy have always been a part of Israel's experience (as indeed of all people), not until the second century B.C.E. did the Hebrews begin to image those events systematically into dualistic images—into terms of a titanic struggle between the agents of darkness and the angels of light, between Satan and God.[2]

The Powers of Darkness

We know from New Testament research that the duel between the forces of Light and the powers of Darkness is firmly rooted in the literature of the period. Both Apocryphal and Pseudepigraphical writings speak of demons, fallen angels, and Satanic powers which enslave, afflict, tyrannize, maim, and kill. These stories about the triumph of the righteous have offered daily encouragement for those who have felt at the mercy of chaotic forces threatening to sweep them away. The book of Tobit, for example (second century B.C.E.), tells a story about God's help for the Jews in the dispersion. Tobit, a poor, blind Jew from Nineveh, sent his son Tobias back home to Media for money on deposit there. By chance his journey was to bring him in contact with a beautiful young woman, distantly related, whose name was Sarah. Although they met and came to love each other the challenge of the demon remained a threat. The story ended happily, however, when assisted by the angel Raphael and equipped with a magical potion Tobias repulsed the demon and took Sarah for his wife (6:13–17). This simple story has had a continuing hold on the imagination of many Jewish people who have felt that they too might receive help from God, an angel, or a magical potion, and have power over demons.

The literature of the period reflects ever and again the mythic search for origins and answers. Even the origins of evil were mythically traced to the primeval time. Both Jubilees and 1 Enoch, for example, claimed to find a secret revelation in the Genesis narrative about the mystery and power of evil. Jubilees (161–140 B.C.E.) offers a commentary on Genesis 1—Exodus 12 drawn from the revelation given to Moses. In this account Noah prays that the malignant spirits, "the watchers," descended from the illicit union of angels and beautiful earthly maidens (Gen. 6:1–8), might be forbidden to tyrannize the righteous. Yahweh answers the prayer, binding all of the demonic spirits except for a tenth left under the command of Satan to corrupt and lead astray (Jub. 10:5–13). According to Jubilees these rebellious spirits compounded evil upon the earth, seducing humanity into idolatry and war, transgressions, and uncleanliness (11:1–6). Similarly, 1 Enoch (second century B.C.E.) blames violence and the dark arts of magic and astrology on the demons. According to Enoch's revelation, "Azazel [chief of the rebellious angels] taught men to make swords, and knives, and shields . . . and there arose much godlessness" (8:1–2,3). Elsewhere we learn "the spirits of the [evil] giants afflict, oppress, destroy, attack, do battle, and work destruction on the earth, and cause trouble. . . . And then spirits shall rise up against the children of men and against women" (15:11–12).

Evil, with its primeval beginnings, stood as the antithesis of good. Even traditional Hebraic cosmology conforms to this dualistic outlook. God reserves the fiery pit below for the devil and his hosts, the rebel angels, and all other enemies of righteousness, while he prepares the heavens above for the community of the faithful. This cosmology mythically reinforces the belief in the future reversal of present roles. The righteous sufferers, the faithful believers, will find peace and joy while the powerful and the wicked will suffer an annihilating reversal.

The Dead Sea Scrolls also shared the Jewish apocalyptic vision of a violent struggle between God and the hostile powers for world dominion. Yet the Scrolls went beyond this vision to define the role the community must play in the "last days." The presence of evil defined the mission of the sect.

The angel of darkness allied with all of the "sons of wickedness" challenged the dominion of the "prince of lights" (*1 QS* 3:18–21), leading astray the children of light and causing them to stumble (*1 QS* 3:21–25). Belial, the chief of demons, oppressed the faithful (*1 QS* 3:24), dealing them punishing blows (*1 QS* 4:12). From the ravages of these demented warriors the community provided sanctuary and the resources of the law to steel the Qumraners for the struggle. While the community offered shelter from demons prowling outside the camp, expulsion from the sacred circle exposed the victim to the terrors of an evil society and the frightful assault of Belial's minions. Moreover, this cosmic struggle raged in microcosm in the breast of each member of the community. As the Scroll of the Rule tells us, "Till now the Spirits of truth and perversity battle in the hearts of every man. . . . For God has allotted these (spirits) in equal parts until the final end, the time of Renewal" (IV:23, 24).

Much of the New Testament shares fully in the mythology of evil of its Jewish parent. Except for Messiah Jesus the actors in the cosmic drama are the same—Michael, a powerful champion of Israel, contests the devil's claim to the body of Moses (Jude 9; see Rev. 12:7; Dan. 12:1; Jub. 1:29, et al.). Beliar (more correctly Belial), the prince of darkness, challenges Christ (2 Cor. 6:15; see Test. of Levi 3:3; 18:12; Ascension of Isa. 4:2; *1 QS* 1:18; CD 4:13; *1 QH* 3:27, 39, et al.). Satan (Mark 1:13; 4:15; 8:33; Rom. 16:20, et al.), or "the god of this world," (2 Cor. 4:4), along with his multitudes and unclean spirits, opposes all forces of righteousness and children of light. To this array of evil personalities Paul adds Sin and Death as active cosmic threats. While the personalities are the same, the New Testament chronology is slightly different. Here the timetable announcing the beginning of the decisive conflict between the God of creation and the evil titans is moved up. The life, death, and resurrection of Jesus signals the arrival of God's rule designed to dethrone Satan from his seat of power. Although New Testament writers believe God in the Jesus event had wounded Satan, the victory though certain is not yet complete.

The fellowship of those "in Christ," like the Qumran community and hellenistic Jewish congregations, feared the snares of the demonic. They also experienced the intensity of the conflict between God and the apostles of discord. Like their Jewish contemporaries New Testament authors distinguish between the followers of Satan, "children of darkness" (1 Thess. 5:5; *1 QS* 3:19–25), and the disciples of the Lord, or "children of light" (John 12:36; *1 QS* 1:9–11; 3:13, 24–25). The space occupied by evil is the same— demons work under cover of darkness, live in cemeteries, inhabit unclean animals, use the sea as their lair. (Actually, from the third millennium on, beginning with the Sumerian myth of Creation [Enuma Elish],[3] ancient

Near Eastern myths describe the sea as evil, harboring mythic monsters and agents of chaos.)

Using these mythic conventions the Gospel of Mark includes a fascinating story about a demoniac who lived night and day among the unclean tombs, frustrating all efforts to restrain him and screaming his delirious cries into the night. Jesus exorcised this legion of demons, who then took refuge in a nearby herd of swine, by nature unclean; the demons then stampeded the swine into the sea—a natural habitat for demons.

The Pauline letters likewise share a dualistic mythology. The Apostle believes that the dominance of Satan contributes to the instability of this world (1 Cor. 7:31; 2 Cor. 4:4). Death and Sin along with their hired servants join other evil agents to battle God for control of the world. Momentarily the evil forces are in ascendancy; the rulers of this world-age and their subjects, says Paul, crucified the "Lord of glory" and continue to resist the Creator (1 Cor. 2:6–8). Although free for the moment to waste and destroy, these evil powers would soon meet their demise in the approaching denouement (Rom. 6:23; 1 Cor. 15:26, 55). Both evil angels and demonic principalities seek to isolate the believer from the love of God (Rom. 8:38–39). Active at pagan religious feasts, demons attempt to wean away from the table of Christ those believers who share the sacred feasts of "pagans" (1 Cor. 10:20–22). The devil takes advantage of human weakness (1 Cor. 7:5) and seeks advantage over the Apostle and the church (2 Cor. 2:11). This cosmic myth dominates both the view of the future and the interpretation of the past of much first-century Jewish religion and early Christianity.

Although these instruments of darkness evoked awful dread, communities of faith and even individuals were far from defenseless. Under the umbrella of popular myth, magic spells, amulets, holy disciplines, and holy men warded off or exorcised these demonic forces. In the ancient Near East this power of darkness had no abstract locus. Instead this power was gathered up in a political structure, a cosmic system, an evil personality, or a deranged human being; its manifestation was almost always personal and its remedy nearly always concrete. Judaism held that all persons were subjects of some power or mythos. Consequently an autonomous existence was inconceivable. The question was hardly whether a person would be subject to a power but which power one chose to serve—whether it brought hurt or healing, fullness or emptiness, life or death, salvation or destruction.

In his encyclopaedic treatment of Jewish symbols, E.R. Goodenough shows how many thought that amulets sewn to the robes of priests, worn on clothing, attached to door posts, or inscribed on tombs protected against evil powers. Even the *tefillin* worn on the arm and forehead may have functioned as a magic charm. (*Tefillin* were miniature boxes containing the Scripture prescribing their use.) A third century C.E. tradition has Rabbi

Johanan wear the *tefillin* as a talisman against evil spirits. Goodenough believes certain grave decorations—lions, fish, wine cups, wreaths, etc.—were meant to protect the deceased from an evil environment.[4]

While much of Goodenough's evidence involves later periods and is therefore not directly relevant to the question of New Testament origins, surely his central point is valid: in amulets, divinations, and sorcery (e.g., Deut. 18:9–14), the Israelites used those magical symbols and practiced those magical arts which offered protection in an uncertain, hostile, or capricious environment. We may assume the prohibition of the use of amulets and charms was necessary only because so many employed them.

Second Maccabees 12:32–45 offers literary support for Goodenough's archeologically based thesis. Judas Maccabeus found what he took to be the cause of a severe battlefield setback in the "tokens of the idols of Jamnia" some soldiers had concealed under their clothing. In time of war, however, soldiers may understandably resort to unorthodox methods of protection, even when forbidden. Goodenough correctly notes the use of the Catholic St. Christopher medal in World War II by Jewish and Protestant soldiers alike.

In other cases the line between the use of magic and divinely sanctioned power is not always so well defined.[5] Josephus, for example, knew of a root that rids the one possessed of evil spirits (*War* 7:185); the Essenes as well showed an intense interest in ancient books dealing with cures wrought by medicinal roots and stones (*War* 2:163). Elsewhere we see amulets inscribed with the sacred name of Moses and with mythic images (e.g., the snake), used by both Jews and Gentiles to secure magical protection against threatening, demonic elements.[6] Although disputing a number of Goodenough's points, John Gager does agree, "the direct and active participation of Jews in the syncretistic milieu which produced the magical documents" must be assumed.[7]

The Holy Man

Although many felt charms, formulas, and names successfully repelled evil, it was the holy man, suffused with the power and substance of the gods, commissioned by the community to control or expel evil forces, who most often gave these remedies their power. Charged with sustaining the aspirations of the people and troubled by their anxieties, the holy man came to unburden the oppressed, console the desperate, heal the sick, and rescue the humble poor from their plight and degradation.[8] As God's champion and custodian of the secrets of magical powers, this holy figure was both isolated from the community yet servant to it. He held powers others feared; he actively challenged dangerous, destructive spirits, taking enormous risks. In this sense the presence of the holy man in a community was an electrifying experience, sparking off fierce resistance in his confrontation with the demonic. Thus the community joyously welcomed the holy man, for his coming promised relief from the tyranny of evil.

Traditions about such miracle workers were deeply embedded in Israel's memory. Moses had beaten the Egyptian magicians at their own game. Elijah miraculously multiplied a supply of meal (1 Kings 17:8–16), raised the dead (1 Kings 17:17–24), and made brackish water potable (2 Kings 1:19–22). Similarly, Elisha increased a supply of oil (2 Kings 4:1–7) and raised a dead child (2 Kings 4:25–37). These and similar traditions provoked later speculation about miracle workers, emphasizing mythological elements from a much later period which were commonly refracted back onto them.

In the Genesis Apocryphon from Qumran, for example, the Pharaoh became deathly ill after forcing Sarah into a union with himself. Despite feverish efforts by the Egyptian sorcerers he grew steadily worse. After Abraham prayed and laid his hands on the Pharaoh, though, "the scourge departed from him and the evil [Spirit] was rebuked away [from him], and he recovered" (20:16–19). Abraham's power to expel evil spirits reflected mythic elements from the second century B.C.E., rather than from the second millennium to which Abraham historically belonged.

Similarly, from cave four at Qumran comes a fragment about Daniel's healing of King Nebuchadnezzar of Babylon. The king says, "I was afflicted with an ulcer for seven years . . . and a *Gazer* [i.e., an exorcist or magician] pardoned my sins."⁹ This portrayal of Daniel as an exorcist postdates the book of Daniel by perhaps a century. This anachronism quite possibly reflects a growing anxiety of this later time about evil spirits and a confidence that a divinely empowered figure like Daniel could offer protection against such spirits.

Although from the second century B.C.E. onwards most viewed the miraculous powers of holy men in light of these and other biblical notables, Moses stood above all others as a divine figure with miracle-working powers. The speculation about Moses was present at all levels of first-century Judaism from the thoroughly hellenized Philo to the Dead Sea sectarians, from Josephus to the anonymous authors of the Pseudepigraphic materials.

As early as the second century B.C.E., Ben Sirach (or Ecclesiasticus) linked the glory of God that set Moses' face aglow with his mighty works (45:2–3). In *Biblical Antiquities* of pseudo-Philo (70–100 C.E.), God predicts before Moses' birth that he will be an instrument of his wonder-working powers (9:7; see also 9:10 and 12:2). Artapanus, a hellenized Jew from Egypt, tells how Moses, after his miraculous release from prison, barged into the Pharaoh's bed chamber and woke the sleeping king. Responding to the king's demand to know the name of Israel's God, Moses whispered the sacred, ineffable name in the ear of the king who immediately fell dead and was then revived by Moses. Although this passage deals with Moses' triumph over Egyptian oppression and his superiority over Egyptian gods, heroes, and culture,[10] it was relevant nevertheless to Moses' powers as a holy man that he was well equipped for the struggle with all kinds of oppression, including the demonic.

At Qumran we see how well this holy man, Moses, interfaces with an apocalyptic outlook. Since the rules of the sect protected the community from powers of darkness, its members praise God that "during the dominion of Belial and amid the mysteries of his hostility they have not driven [us] from Thy Covenant" (1 QM 14:9–10). Concerning the self-imposed discipline the community says, "This is what they [i.e., the sectarians] shall do, year by year, during all the time of Belial" (1 QS 2:19). Just as Moses was raised up by the "Prince of Light" to save Israel from Belial in the wilderness wandering, so now the community believed that the Teacher of Righteousness leads the community into a wilderness habitat separated from an evil society and gives it an interpretation of the law for resisting Belial.[11]

It was Philo, however, who gave the most comprehensive interpretation of Moses. Philo was a wealthy, politically influential, well-educated Jew who lived in Alexandria from about 15 B.C.E. to 45 C.E. As a prolific writer and cosmopolitan figure, Philo aimed to convince the Diaspora Jew embarrassed by his Hebrew religion that his faith was superior to the dominant hellenistic religion. Philo sought to drape his hero in the colorful attire of Hellenism without producing a grotesque caricature of his subject or a fatal compromise of his Jewish tradition. His portrait of Moses depicted a true cosmopolitan-born Chaldean possessing astrological and magical secrets, accomplished in wisdom as an Egyptian, an esteemed philosopher from whom Plato derived his thought, an ascetic, a prophet, and a divine man.

Philo incorporated in Moses the robustness of every culture he knew. Possessing all the qualities of an ideal Greek figure, says Philo, Moses was the perfect model of "self restraint, continence, temperance, shrewdness, knowledge, endurance of toil and hardships, contempt of pleasures, justice, advocacy of excellence, censure . . . for wrong doers . . . praise and honor for the just" (*The Life of Moses* I, 154). Not only was Moses a friend and pupil of God, being taught "face to face" (*Moses* I, 80), he was also in some sense divine himself. Recalling Exodus 7:1, "See, I make you as God to Pharaoh," Philo spoke of Moses as a "*theios-aner*," or god-man (*Virtues* 177), capable of performing signs and wonders (see Deut. 34:10–12). Even though Philo gave the preeminent place in Moses' character to virtue his wonder working powers clearly aimed to authenticate his divine status.[12]

Moses' knowledge of the divine name gave him power over the Pharaoh and the Egyptian priests and, as Tiede has shown, demonstrated his superiority to Egyptian culture.[13] Linked with the patriarchs (Abraham, Isaac, Jacob, and Joseph), Moses surpassed them all in communion with God and in possession of the godly *Logos*—that divine principle of reason permeating and governing all creation. This divine *Logos* inspired and informed Moses' status as king and god of creation, lawgiver, high priest, prophet, miracle worker, ascetic, and philosopher (*Moses* I, 158; II, 187–292; II, 1–186). Alive with these divine gifts Moses was a fitting rival for any hellenistic sage or holy man.

In many ways Philo's image of Moses resembles Philostratus' portrait of Apollonius of Tyana, a hellenistic holy man from the first century. Although Philostratus' biography was late (3d century C.E.), most scholars see in it traditions and forms of piety shared with much of first-century religious expression.

Like Philo's Moses Apollonius was an ascetic. Abstaining from wine and meat and following a celibate rule, Apollonius wore only garments of linen ("earthwool") thus sparing the animals. Renouncing wealth and embracing periods of silence up to five years (!) Apollonius abandoned this world and its distractions for the divine. From Egypt to India, from Asia Minor to Rome, Apollonius preached, taught, and worked miracles. In Philostratus' biography, we find him predicting a plague, healing a boy bitten by a "mad dog," raising a little girl from the dead, and stopping a bread riot. Like Jesus, Apollonius frequently engaged and controlled demons. Once, for example, he heeded the pitiful plea of a mother who spoke of the angry threats of a demon to hurl her over a cliff and to murder her demon possessed son if she sought exorcism. Apollonius predictably expelled the demon and restored the young man to sanity through a letter threatening the "ghost" (III, 38).

In another instance, we are told, he stopped a plague by urging the Ephesians to stone an old blind man whom only Apollonius recognized as a demon. He who seemed blind before turned into a glaring, crazed demon with eyes ablaze when challenged by Apollonius. When the Ephesians realized this was a demon they showered him with stones expelling the evil spirit. Under the heap they later found a corpse, not of a blind man but of a mad dog (IV, 10). Elsewhere, demons causing drunkenness cried out in fear and hostility whenever Apollonius approached (IV, 20).

Even from these brief sketches we can see the variety in types of holy men described in the relevant materials. Neither Philo's Moses nor Philostratus' Apollonius is precisely like Jesus, and yet there are similarities. Few would question the widespread belief in the first century that divine men existed and did mighty works. While neither Philo's Moses nor Philostratus' Apollonius perform in the charged atmosphere of apocalypticism, their status as divine men with miracle working powers illumines New Testament patterns even if it does not explain them. The mythic lens through which Philo and Philostratus viewed their world offered a vision of the human that was fully cosmopolitan, inspired with the divine, and attuned to Greek philosophical categories. The lens filtered out any eschatological coloration of time, bringing into focus instead the sharp contours of space. This vision of Philo in particular was more cerebral, less traditionally ethical, and almost entirely lacking in the apocalyptic emphases we see elsewhere.

As at Qumran where Moses' wonder-working powers were placed in an apocalytpic frame, the Synoptic Gospels all tend to associate Jesus' miracle-working powers with the proclamation of the kingdom of God, a fresh application of an old apocalyptic expression. The Gospel of Mark, for example, lays in tandem Jesus' contest with Satan in the temptation narrative (1:13), John's announcement of the arrival of the kingdom of God (1:14–15), Jesus' teaching with authority (1:21–22) and the *first* miracle Jesus performs, an exorcism (1:23–28)! Thus Mark's arrangement links the mighty works of Jesus with the final apocalyptic struggle between the demonic forces and God.

In the ministry of Jesus, a powerful worker of wonders, God is exercising his lordship over the creation. After a brief interlude, the healing of Peter's mother-in-law, come two accounts of massive exorcisms (1:32, 34; 1:39). In 3:14–15 Jesus commissions the disciples, giving them authority over demons, and in 3:20–27 Jesus disputes the accusation of expelling demons in the name of the prince of demons. Such a view, Jesus maintains, is a contradiction, for "if a kingdom is divided against itself, that kingdom cannot stand"(3:24). Luke and Matthew make explicit the Marcan tendency to associate the proclamation of the kingdom of God with Jesus' exorcisms: "If it is by the finger of God that I cast out demons, then the kingdom of God has come upon you"(Luke 11:20; parallel Matt. 12:28).

Although their experience with evil was real and terrifying, few Jews (including Jewish Messianists) believed the dualism between evil and holy powers was absolute. In the exorcist's authority over demons many would have seen a bold manifestation of God's sovereignty over the world. The Gospel narratives about demons, then, dealt not only with troublesome issues in the idiom of the day, these exorcisms also legitimized the title "Lord" given to Jesus. His power to command the demons established Jesus' credentials as Messiah, offering hope and consolation to a people oppressed and promising relief from mysterious, destructive powers.

The mental picture of demons inhabiting swine, or causing spontaneous, delirious cries, or attacking and killing hapless victims, or engaging Jesus in live conversation may strike us as bizarre. The remedies offered—the use of charms, names, magical formulas, community sanctuary, or powers of a holy man—may also strain credulity. The skeptic may dismiss these conventions of language and outlook as superstition, just as the embarrassed believer may strain to ignore these odd configurations. But as we better understand these expressions we are more able to understand the intent of the Gospels, letters, and the Apocalypse, and perhaps our own tortured world as well. A sensitive, but not uncritical reading of this strange idiom may reveal some of the frustration and fear of a people caught in a dark web closing in on them, some of the desperation of having one's destiny dictated by powers beyond one's comprehension or control, or some of the sense of helplessness and abandonment of a people to whom evil seemed more immediate, more real, than God's power or sovereignty over the world.

Now that we come to the end of our study, what can we say in summary? If one were to enter a time capsule and return to first-century Judah or some other part of the hellenistic world, what would one see? Would Judah, a small, remote, and rather weak Roman province, assume the significance it has come to have in the Judaeo-Christian tradition? Probably not. Would one notice Jewish institutions struggling to retain the integrity of their symbols, functionaries, and teachings against the steady erosion of Hellenism and Roman attempts to undermine or compromise them? That is unlikely also. Would one pay attention to a group of ill-equipped, untrained, yet fervent revolutionaries challenging the Roman legions? That is even more improbable.

Would one feel the weight of internal squabbles and heated debates between priests devoted to the temple and alienated Essenes and Jewish Messianists? That could easily escape notice. If we should visit a synagogue or gathering of followers of Jesus would we be persuaded by their methods of Scripture interpretation? The points of distinction might be too fine for us. We might be struck by the way popular piety dealt with an environment dark and foreboding and sought to make some simple affirmations in the face of those realities, but the dimensions of this struggle might elude us as well.

Although the distance between us and the first century places us at a great disadvantage, making it necessary to work with only scattered clues in order to attempt to reconstruct that world, hindsight has some advantages. We are in a better position to see certain forces at work shaping Judaism and early Christianity than were contemporaries of the events described here. The later trajectory of history has made it easier to follow the early course of events. We are able to look synoptically at the internal dynamism of this movement and the external religious, political, social, and economic forces shaping the movement from which the New Testament came. Our understanding, however limited, of that world in which the New Testament was formed and with which it was engaged in active dialogue should assist the text in speaking with its own voice.

If we pause to survey the path traveled thus far one point is clear. The New Testament authors wrote from *inside* their world; they had no alternative. They appropriated from and interacted with their total environment.

Yet it is inappropriate to say they *borrowed* from it, if by borrowing one means the authors discretely took from a store of images, texts, rhetorical devices, and myths to frame their documents, as if their social and cultural environment were only a grab-bag from which they selected symbols to construct a reality that people would believe. Such a view places the authors outside the world they inhabited and assumes the audience was a passive receptacle rather than a cultural cohort in lively conversation with the author.

The term "borrowing" calls to mind the image of a modern scholar divorced from the world studied, eclectically taking from a library of resources to form an opinion or rationally assess a problem. New Testament authors were hardly propagandists who manipulated cultural and social conventions to frame a political, economic, or religious ideology. Such an understanding tends to divorce the authors from their context and ascribe to them critical methods more at home in our world than theirs. Historians today generally prefer the verbs "to incorporate" and "to appropriate" over the more prejudicial verb "to borrow." Such verbs more accurately describe a process that was less conscious on their part than it is descriptive of the inclusive interaction between the author and the available vocabularies of thought, culture, and tradition he shared with his readers.

The interaction with the world is a dynamic process. A flash of insight, a holy figure, or a historical event pregnant with meaning may lead an author to view the world in a new way. Through this transvaluation traditions, Scriptures, or established symbols may be so intensely focused that their message may become that much more compelling. Flashes of insight may generate new symbols, inspire new visions of the future, and at the same time destabilize patterns judged secure, injecting ferment into existing structures. Such change may generate excitement and protest in some circles and stubborn resistance in others. The New Testament is a record of such a process.

The word *process* is chosen deliberately because the writings are not the end product of a pilgrimage of thought or belief but a snapshot in the course of self-discovery, self-definition, and self-understanding of a real community. Through the mythological lens with which our authors viewed the world and through the sociological, historical lens with which we view their landscape, a new perspective of the whole is gained; the whole taken together reveals to us an enriched understanding of each part.

The integrating center of the New Testament is the proclamation that Jesus is the Christ. It was that belief which influenced the way the New Testament authors envisioned the world, and the world itself that gave the church its language for expressing that belief. For that reason we have included discussions of the major realities of the first-century New Testament writers—political history, and a treatment of institutions, forms of religious expression, scriptural interpretation, and the mythical significance of evil.

As limited as these discussions have been they are all important because they are integral to the world which shaped the Christian consciousness. One plane cannot easily be severed from any other, because all interact and all are reflected in microcosm in the New Testament itself. The better we are able to imagine the New Testament in its natural setting, the easier it will be to understand what the debates there are about—questions reaching beyond their own time: can a people find release from the forces that swept and even now sweep through history like an avalanche? Is there a caring will at the heart of the universe? Can a fractured world be healed? If so, how?

These same questions which were significant for all those who experienced the events of the New Testament are still asked today. We too may ponder the words written in the Bible searching for wise answers to these timeless questions, hoping for an understanding of the forces shaping our common history and framing our present, and craving a fuller comprehension and appreciation of our culture informed by the biblical story.

In one sense, though, the words we find there are coded—coded by the relationship of those words to a different cultural matrix than the one in which we live. Like any code, though, these words can still be made to speak to us—if only we can find the right key.

Notes

CHAPTER 1

1. W.W. Tarn, *Alexander the Great* (Boston: Beacon Press, 1956), 145.
2. Ibid., 145–147.
3. Ibid., 147–148.
4. Other sources claim that he simply removed the pole pin holding the knot and took it apart.
5. Arrian, *Anabasis of Alexander*, trans. by P.A. Brunt, Loeb Classical Library Series (Cambridge: Harvard University Press, 1976), III.4.5.
6. Ibid., III.26.4.
7. Some suspect they were lovers. J.R. Hamilton, *Alexander the Great* (London: Hutchinson University Library, 1973), 145.
8. Ibid., 145.
9. See Victor Tcherikover, *Hellenistic Civilization and the Jews*, A Temple Book, (New York: Atheneum, 1970), 188.
10. Unless otherwise noted citations are from Flavius Josephus, *The Jewish War*, trans. by H. St. J. Thackeray, Loeb Classical Library, (Cambridge, Mass.: Harvard University Press, 1976), hereafter *War*. This citation however, is from the translation by G.A. Williamson, *The Jewish War* (New York: Penguin Books, 1978).
11. David M. Rhoads, *Israel in Revolution 6–74 C.E.: A Political History Based on the Writings of Josephus* (Philadelphia: Fortress, 1976), 67–68.
12. Morton Smith, "Zealots and Sicarii: Their Origins and Relation," *Harvard Theological Review*, 64 (1971), 1–19, has an excellent discussion of distinctions which can be drawn between the Zealots and Sicarii.
13. Rhoads, *Israel in Revolution*, 111–122.
14. Nahman Avigad, "Excavations in the Jewish Quarter of the Old City, 1969–1971," *Jerusalem Revealed*, ed. Yigael Yadin (Jerusalem: Israel Exploration Society, 1975), 41–51.
15. *The War Scroll*, commonly referred to as 1 QM. Discussion of this and other documents of the Qumran community will follow in chapter 2.
16. See R.H. Charles, ed., *The Apocrypha and Pseudepigrapha of the Old Testament*, 2 vols. (Oxford: Clarendon Press, 1968), II, 647–651.

CHAPTER 2

1. Jacob Neusner, *The Rabbinic Traditions About the Pharisees Before 70*, 3 vols. (Leiden: E.J. Brill, 1971), III, 247.
2. Jacob Neusner, *From Politics to Piety: The Emergence of Pharisaic Judaism* (Englewood Cliffs, N.J.: Prentice Hall, 1973), 89.

3. See my *The Letters of Paul: Conversations in Context* (Atlanta: John Knox Press, 1982), 14.

4. Unless otherwise noted citations are from Flavius Josephus, *Jewish Antiquities*, trans. by H. St. J. Thackeray, Ralph Marcus, and Louis H. Feldman "Loeb Classical Library" (Cambridge, Mass.: Harvard University Press, 1976). Hereafter *Antiquities*.

5. See Ellis Rivkin, *A Hidden Revolution: The Pharisees' Search for the Kingdom Within* (Nashville: Abingdon, 1978), 72–75, and Neusner, *Rabbinic Traditions*, III, 177.

6. Neusner, *Rabbinic Traditions*, III, 244.

7. Rivkin, *A Hidden Revolution*, 242.

8. Jacob Neusner, "Two Pictures of the Pharisees: Philosophical Circle or Eating Club," *Anglican Theological Review* 64 (1982): 525–538, argues, "the traditions give the impression of intense concentration on the inner life of the party, or sect, whose intimate affairs take precedence, in the larger scheme of history, over the affairs of state, cult, and country" (527). In *A Hidden Revolution*, 176, Rivkin takes the opposite view: "The Pharisees were a scholar class dedicated to the supremacy of the twofold Law, the Written and the Unwritten. They actively opposed the Sadducees who recognized only the Written Law as authoritative, and they sought dramatic means for proclaiming their overriding authority. Their unwritten laws, the *halakhah*, were operative in all realms: cultus, property, judicial procedures, festivals, etc."

9. See my *The Letters of Paul*, 14.

10. A total of fourteen times: Matthew 3:7; 16:1,6,11,12; 22:23,34; Mark 12:18; Luke 20:27; Acts 4:1; 5:17; 23:6,7,8.

11. Joachim Jeremias, *Jerusalem in the Time of Jesus*, trans. F.H. & C.H. Cave (Philadelphia: Fortress, 1969), 236, n. 12, makes too much of the point that Matthew 21:45 has "chief priests and the Pharisees" while Luke 20:9 reads "scribes and chief priests." From this Jeremias concludes that since scribes *and* Pharisees appear nowhere together, the Pharisees on the council were all scribes.

12. Unless noted, all passages are taken from A. Dupont-Sommer, *The Essene Writings from Qumran*, trans. G. Vermes, (Cleveland, Ohio: Meridian Books, World Publishing Co., 1962). The *1* indicates a grouping (cave) number, the *Q*, place of the document's origin, i.e., Qumran, the *S*, the actual document.

13. Here the *C* denotes the place this document was first discovered—Cairo.

14. In this notation, *Q* again refers to the document's origin, *p* indicates the type of document (*pesher*, or commentary), and *Hab*, the book being interpreted—Habakkuk.

15. I realize that the use of "sons" sounds sexist to the modern ear, but only such a translation can accurately reflect the deliberate intentions of the sectarians at Qumran.

16. Martin Hengel, *Was Jesus a Revolutionist?* trans. William Klassen (Philadelphia: Fortress, 1971).

17. As cited by Aharon Oppenheimer, *The 'Am Ha-Aretz: A Study in the Social History of the Jewish People in the Hellenistic-Roman Period*, trans. I.H. Levine (Leiden: E.J. Brill, 1977), 101–102.

18. Ibid., 102.

19. Oppenheimer's thesis, *The 'Am Ha-Aretz*, 228–229, is unconvincing, however, that the Pharisees united with the ʿAm ha-ʾaretz to oppose those "not in full accord with the leadership of the nation," that is Christians, after the destruction of Jerusalem.

20. Gilbert Murray, *Five Stages of Greek Religion* (New York: Doubleday and Co., 1955), 4.
21. See Walter F. Otto, *Dionysus: Myth and Cult*, trans. R.B. Palmer (Bloomington: Indiana University Press, 1965).
22. Edward Vernon Arnold, *Roman Stoicism* (Freeport, N.Y.: Books for Libraries Press [1911] 1971), 86.
23. See my discussion of Apollonius of Tyana, chapter 5.
24. Walter Burkert, *Lore and Science in Ancient Pythagoreanism*, trans. Edwin L. Minar, Jr. (Cambridge, Mass.: Harvard University Press, 1972), 482.
25. Diogenes Laertius, "Diogenes," *Lives of Eminent Philosophers*, trans. R.D. Hicks (London: William Heinemann, 1925), IV, 39.
26. Ibid., VI, 41.
27. Ibid.
28. Seneca, *Ad Lucilium Epistulae Morales*, trans. Richard M. Gummere, Loeb Classical Library (Cambridge, Mass.: Harvard University Press, 1979), V, 21.
29. Hans Dieter Betz, *Der Apostel Paulus und die sokratische Tradition* (Tuebingen: J.C.B. Mohr, 1972), 98.
30. We use gnosticism, lower case, to refer to the proto or pre-gnostic movement reserving Gnosticism, upper case, for the later, definable movement.
31. See my *The Letters of Paul*, 53–62 for a summary.
32. Note especially Guenther Bornkamm, "The Heresy of Colossians," in *Conflict at Colossae: A Problem in the Interpretation of Early Christianity Illustrated by Selected Modern Studies*, ed. and trans. by Fred O. Francis and Wayne A. Meeks (Missoula, Mont.: Scholars Press, 1973), 130.
33. Victor Tcherikover, "The Ideology of the Letter of Aristeas," *Harvard Theological Review* 51 (1958), 81. See also 59–85.
34. Found in *The Apocrypha and Pseudepigrapha of the Old Testament*, ed. R.H. Charles et al. (Oxford: Clarendon Press, 1913), II, sec. 16.
35. John J. Collins, *Between Athens and Jerusalem: Jewish Identity in the Hellenistic Diaspora* (New York: Crossroad, 1983), 51.
36. Salo W. Baron, *A Social and Religious History of the Jews*, 3 vols. (New York: Columbia University Press, 1952), I, 135.
37. Hans Jonas, *Gnostic Religion* (Boston: Beacon Press, 1963), 328.

CHAPTER 3

1. Peter L. Berger and Thomas Luckmann, *The Social Construction of Reality: A Treatise in the Sociology of Knowledge* (Garden City, N.Y.: Doubleday, 1967), 106.
2. Samuel Terrien, "The Omphalos Myth and Hebrew Religion," *Vetus Testamentum* 20 (1970), 315–338. Also see, R.G. Hammerton-Kelly, "The Temple and the Origins of Jewish Apocalyptic," *Vetus Testamentum* 20 (1970), 1–15.
3. Eric M. Meyers and James F. Strange, *Archeology: The Rabbis and Early Christianity* (Nashville: Abingdon, 1981), 52.
4. Mircea Eliade, *The Sacred and the Profane: The Nature of Religion*, trans. Willard R. Trask (New York: Harcourt, Brace and Company, 1958), 59.
5. Ibid.
6. Jacob Neusner, *Judaism: The Evidence of the Mishnah* (Chicago and London: University of Chicago Press, 1981), 228.
7. J.C. Rylaarsdam, "Booths, Feast of," *The Interpreters Dictionary of the Bible* (Nashville: Abingdon, 1962), I, 455–458.
8. Josephus, *Antiquities* III, 186; concerning Philo's interests see E.R. Good-

enough, *By Light, Light: The Mystic Gospel of Hellenistic Judaism* (New Haven: Yale University Press, 1935), 98, 112, 113, 209, et al.

9. Floyd V. Filson, "Temple, Synagogue, Church," *Biblical Archeologist* 7 (1944), 77. See also E.P. Sanders, *Jesus and Judaism* (Philadelphia: Fortress, 1985).

10. See Joseph Gutmann, ed. *Ancient Synagogues: The State of Research*, Brown Judaic Studies 22 (Missoula, Mont.: Scholars Press, 1981). Also note A.T. Kraabel, "The Diaspora Synagogue," *Aufstieg und Niedergang der roemischen Welt*, II Principat, (Berlin, New York: Walter de Gruyter, 1980), 19.1, 500–510.

11. Z. Maʿoz, "The Synagogues of Gamla and the Typology of the Second-Temple Synagogues," *Ancient Synagogues Revealed*, (Jerusalem: The Israel Exploration Society, 1981), esp. 35–41.

12. Philo, *Philo*, trans. F.H. Colson, Loeb Classical Library (Cambridge, Mass.: Harvard University Press, 1966), VI, 557. Citations and translations of Philo are from the Loeb edition unless otherwise noted.

13. Gutmann, *Ancient Synagogues*, 6, 17.

14. The *Birkath-ha-minim* in question runs: "For the renegades let there be no hope, and may the arrogant kingdom soon be rooted out in our days, and the Nazarenes and the minim perish in a moment and be blotted out from the book of life, and with the righteous may they not be inscribed. Blessed art thou, O Lord, who humblest the arrogant."

15. For example, Hans Conzelmann and A. Lindemann, *Arbeitsbuch zum Neuen Testament* (Tuebingen: J.C.B. Mohr [Paul Siebeck], 1980).

16. Trans. and discussed by Herbert G. May, "Synagogues in Palestine," *Biblical Archeologist* 7 (1944), 1–20.

17. Wayne A. Meeks and Robert L. Wilken, *Jews and Christians in Antioch in the First Four Centuries of the Common Era* (Missoula, Mont.: Scholars Press, 1978), 7.

18. Useful discussions of the city in the ancient world may be found in Mason Hammond, *The City in the Ancient World* (Cambridge, Mass.: Harvard University Press, 1972) and Wayne A. Meeks, *The First Urban Christians: The Social World of the Apostle Paul* (New Haven and London: Yale University Press, 1983).

19. As cited in Henri Frankfort, *Ancient Egyptian Religion: An Interpretation* (New York: Columbia University Press, 1948), 54.

20. E.R. Goodenough, "The Political Philosophy of Hellenistic Kingship," *Yale Classical Studies* 1 (1928), ed. Austin M. Harmon, 87–90.

21. Gustav Adolf Deissmann, *Light from the Ancient East*, trans. Lionel R.M. Strachan (Grand Rapids, Mich.: Baker Book House, [1922] 1978), 347.

22. Ibid., 345.

23. Donald L. Jones, "Christianity and the Roman Imperial Cult," *Aufstieg und Niedergang der roemischen Welt*, 23:2, 1026–1027.

24. Ibid., 1035–1036.

25. Adela Yarbro Collins, *Crisis and Catharsis: The Power of the Apocalypse* (Philadelphia: Westminster Press, 1984), 73, holds the view that instead of being a response to Roman persecution Revelation aimed "to awaken and intensify Christian exclusiveness particularly vis-a-vis the imperial cult." The intensification of Christian exclusiveness and the repudiation of the imperial cult, however, are in no way inconsistent with the persecution context assumed here.

26. See Josephus, *Life of Josephus*, trans. H. St. J. Thackeray (Cambridge, Mass.: Harvard University Press, 1976), 244; *War*, 3, 459; *War*, 7, 71.

27. Fred W. Danker, *Benefactor: Epigraphic Study of a Graeco-Roman and New Testament Semantic Field* (St. Louis: Clayton Publishing House, 1982) has the best English study known to me on the term *Benefactor*. His conclusion is that the concept of the "Graeco-Roman benefactor dominates in the presentations of God that are set forth in the New Testament" (p. 493). Whereas God functions as "chief benefactor" Jesus serves as the "endangered benefactor," i.e., through his death God's good will comes to all, Jew and Gentile. Although only Luke uses the term *euergetes* to refer to persons in authority (22:25), Danker believes this offers a conceptual parallel to other literature of the period in its understanding of the term. See the review of Danker's book by David E. Aune in *Interpretation* 38 (1984), 421–425.

CHAPTER 4

1. Charles, ed. *The Apocrypha and Pseudepigrapha of the Old Testament*, II, 83–122.
2. H.M. Orlinsky, "The Treatment of Anthropomorphisms and Anthropopathisms in the Septuagint of Isaiah," *Hebrew Union College Annual* 27 (1956), 193–200, quite properly cautions against overgeneralizing. The text of the Septuagint is inconsistent. In some cases anthropomorphisms are tolerated; in others, smoothed or removed.
3. It would be a mistake to assume that the text of the Septuagint was stable. From the beginning there were attempts to modify the LXX to make it conform more closely to the Hebrew text. Finally, the insistence of the Letter of Aristeas (2d century, B.C.E.) on the divinely inspired character of the Greek translation is defensive: "Since the translation in its beautiful, devout, and utterly exact form is complete, it is right and proper that it should be preserved in this wording and not undergo any change." This apologetic statement was aimed at those who questioned the adequacy of the Septuagint. We know of no serious reservations about the integrity of the Septuagint in the Diaspora Judaism of the first century. In adopting the Septuagint as its Bible, the church likewise harbored no doubts about the veracity of the text. In the second and third centuries C.E. other editions or rescensions of the LXX appear once again. Concerning the Septuagintal influence on Paul, see A.D. Nock, "The Vocabulary of the New Testament," *Journal of Biblical Literature* 52 (1933), 138–139, reprinted in *Essays on Religion and the Ancient World*, ed. Zeph Stewart, 2 vols. (Cambridge, Mass.: Harvard University Press, 1972), I, 346–347.
4. Samuel Sandmel, *Philo of Alexandria: An Introduction* (New York, Oxford: Oxford University Press, 1979), 123.
5. See also Ephesians 2:15 which speaks of Christ's creating in himself "one new man in place of two," an apparent allusion to the reconciliation of the earthly and heavenly "man." For a fuller discussion see my "Jewish Christian—Gentile Christian Relations: A Discussion of Ephesians 2:15a," *Zeitschrift für die Neutestamentliche Wissenschaft* 74 (1983), 87–88. Also germane is Robin Scrogg's *The Last Adam* (Philadelphia: Fortress, 1966).
6. See Philo's "The Preliminary Studies," in *Philo*, Loeb Classical Library, IV, 451–551.
7. Allegory as used by Philo, Paul, and Mark is often treated pejoratively. James Barr, *Old and New in Interpretation* (London: SCM Press, 1964), 103–148, however, has captured for us the positive side.
8. Geza Vermes, *Scripture and Tradition in Judaism* (Leiden: E.J. Brill, 1961), 178.

9. Exceptions such as the "War Scroll" which deals with the final eschatological war, the "Copper Scroll" which encodes the location of buried treasure, and "The Manual of Discipline" which treats the initiatory rites, regulation of communal life, and some beliefs nuclear to community should be recalled.

10. Geza Vermes, "The Qumran Interpretation of Scripture in Its Historical Setting," *Leeds University Oriental Society Annual* 6 (1966–68), 86–87 and 88–97. A lucid, useful treatment is also available in F.F. Bruce, *Biblical Exegesis in the Qumran Texts* (Grand Rapids: Eerdmans, 1959), and in William H. Brownlee, "Biblical Interpretation Among the Sectaries of the Dead Sea Scrolls," *The Biblical Archeologist* 14 (1951), 54–76.

11. Bruce, *Biblical Exegesis in the Qumran Texts.*

12. See Brownlee, "Biblical Interpretation."

13. See Vermes, *Scripture and Tradition in Judaism,* 26–39.

14. I realize the difficulty of using the term Midrash. Its precise meaning in the first century is a matter of continuing study. I use it, nevertheless, with reservations for the sake of convenience.

15. Especially helpful is Geza Vermes, "The Qumran Interpretation of Scripture in Its Historical Setting," 84–97. By the same author is "At Qumran and in the Targums," listed under "Interpretation, History of" in *The Interpreters Dictionary of the Bible: Supplementary Volume* (Nashville: Abingdon, 1976), 438–443.

16. Geza Vermes, "Jewish Literature and New Testament Exegesis: Reflections on Methodology," *Journal of Jewish Studies* 33 (1982), 1–2, 361–376.

17. David Daube "Rabbinic Methods of Interpretation and Hellenistic Rhetoric," *Hebrew Union College Annual* 22 (1949), 239–264.

18. Other guides allow one to draw similar inferences by analogy. For example, it is assumed that a slave must be set free if abused. If, for instance, a master blinds a servant in one eye or knocks out a permanent tooth, the slave must be freed. Similarly, it was reasoned, a slave if deprived of the use of any member which, like the eye or tooth, cannot regenerate itself, must be set free although the law explicitly mentions only the eye and the tooth. A useful discussion is available in J.W. Doeve, *Jewish Hermeneutics in the Synoptic Gospels and Acts* (Assen: Van Gorcum and Comp, 1954), 67–68.

19. See my *The Letters of Paul,* 15–16. The seventh and final rule of Hillel sought to solve certain scriptural puzzles by reading the text in context (*Dabhar Hallamedh Me'Inyano*). For example, the commandment "Thou shalt not steal" was interpreted to refer to the stealing of human beings (i.e., kidnapping), because the commandments preceding and following this one both forbid crimes against another person (i.e., murder and adultery). I know of no such usage in the New Testament.

20. This term refers to the ancient practice of using one "type" to illumine another. For example, in Romans 5:12–21 Paul sees the first Adam as a type of Adam who was to come, viz., the Messiah Jesus.

CHAPTER 5

1. See my "Paul and His Myths," *The Letters of Paul,* 81–92.

2. Frank M. Cross, *Canaanite Myth and Hebrew Epic* (Cambridge, Mass.: Harvard University Press, 1973), pointed to the cosmogonic myth in the Psalms in which a struggle between the agent of evil and Yahweh is described. Not until a later period, however, do we see the systematic development here noted.

3. James B. Pritchard, *Ancient Near Eastern Texts* (Princeton: Princeton University Press, 1955), 60–72. This point is well made also by Adela Yarbro Collins, *The*

Combat Myth and the Book of Revelation (Missoula, Mont.: Scholars Press, 1976).

4. E.R. Goodenough, *Jewish Symbols in the Greco-Roman Period* (New York: Pantheon Books, 1964), II, 216.

5. David E. Aune, "Magic in Early Christianity," *Aufstieg und Niedergang der roemischen Welt*, eds. Hildegard Temporini and Wolfgang Haase (Berlin, New York: Walter de Gruyter, 1980), II, 23.2, 1507–1557.

6. John Gager, *Moses in Greco-Roman Paganism* (Nashville, New York: Abingdon Press, 1972), 146–159.

7. Ibid., 160.

8. Peter Brown's seminal article, "The Rise and Function of the Holy Man in Late Antiquity," *Journal of Roman Studies* 21 (1971), 80–101, deals with figures of a later period, but contains, nevertheless, much that is valuable for students of the first century. Also useful is Otto Boecher's, *Daemonenfurcht und Daemonenabwehr* (Stuttgart: Verlag W. Kohlhammer, 1970).

9. "The Prayer of Nabonibus," found in A. Dupont-Sommer, *The Essene Writings From Qumran*, 322–323.

10. David L. Tiede, *The Charismatic Figure as Miracle Worker* (Missoula: Scholars Press, 1972), 177.

11. Ibid., 190–193.

12. Ibid., 107–110.

13. Ibid., 168.

Index